STEVE MIZERAK'S
WINNING
POCKET BILLIARDS

STEVE MIZERAK'S
WINNING
POCKET BILLIARDS

WITH JOEL H. COHEN

Contemporary Books, Inc.
Chicago

Library of Congress Cataloging in Publication Data

Mizerak, Steve, 1944–
  Steve Mizerak's Winning pocket billiards.

  Includes index.
  1. Pool (Game)   I. Cohen, Joel H.   II. Title.
III. Title: Winning pocket billiards.
GV891.M694   1984   794.7'3   84-9622
ISBN 0-8092-5777-7

Caricatures are by Brian Katz.

Photography is by Ken Lonky, taken at
the Four Seasons Billiard Lounge,
Metuchen, New Jersey, owned by
John Sabara and John Javadi.

Published by Contemporary Books, Inc.
180 North Michigan Avenue, Chicago, Illinois 60601
Manufactured in the United States of America
Library of Congress Catalog Card Number: 84-9622
International Standard Book Number: 0-8092-5777-7

Published simultaneously in Canada by Beaverbooks, Ltd.
195 Allstate Parkway, Valleywood Business Park
Markham, Ontario L3R 4T8 Canada

To the Miller Brewing Company, which made my career,
and to my wife, Karen, who made me what I am today

CONTENTS

INTRODUCTION   ix

1 EQUIPPING YOURSELF TO ADVANCE   **1**

2 FINDING YOUR OWN STYLE   **21**

3 GAME PLANS   **41**

4 YOU'RE NEVER TOO GOOD TO
LEARN   **57**

5 THE BIG TEST   **73**

6 POOLROOM CHARACTER TYPES:
WHICH OF THEM IS YOU?   **137**

7 TOURNAMENTS I'VE PLAYED
AND LESSONS I'VE LEARNED   **159**

ABOUT STEVE MIZERAK   **171**

INDEX   **177**

INTRODUCTION

The longer I play pool, the more I realize how much there is to learn. Everybody—not only beginners, but intermediate and advanced players, and even champions—can always pick up an idea to help his or her game along.

Even though I've won four U.S. Open championships and scores of other pocket billiards titles, I regularly experience something that's worth storing in my memory bank to draw on when I'm at the pool table. Sometimes it's a lesson that comes from a mistake that I've made or that my opponent has made. Sometimes it's the way another player deals with a particular situation or problem at the table. Often it's a mental or psychological factor I haven't considered before. Whatever the source, though, these pointers are useful to me as a means of elevating my game another notch.

In this book I'm going to share with you some of the things I've learned along the way. I'm assuming that you've already mastered the fundamentals of pocket pool and possibly some of the other games played on the pool table as well. So I'm not going to dwell on the basics, but rather give a brief overview of the ever-important fundamentals, recognizing that even in that area there are tips to help a player improve.

Another assumption is that you're eager to improve the caliber of your play so that you can start winning more consistently and possibly move up to a higher level of competition.

Accordingly, I'm going to discuss a variety of subjects from the standpoint of showing you how to become a more advanced player. Starting with equipment selection and care, I'll cover mental and physical mistakes to avoid and proper strategy and execution in specific situations in Straight Pool, Nine-Ball, Eight-Ball, and One-Pocket. Based on my years of experience, I'll describe poolroom character types that may remind you (fortunately or unfortunately) of yourself. And I'll tell you about some of the most exciting, important matches I've had the privilege of participating in (winning some, losing some), emphasizing what you and I can learn from those experiences.

Obviously, reading this book and absorbing the lessons doesn't guarantee that you'll improve as a pocket pool player. But if you put these principles into practice *at the table,* I'm confident you will get better.

Remember the old joke about the little old lady who wants to feed chicken soup to the actor who has just collapsed on stage? ("He's dead, madam; it won't help," says the manager, to which the woman replies, "It couldn't hurt.") The advice in this book won't hurt you; it should help and maybe even entertain you.

Good luck with your game!

STEVE MIZERAK'S
WINNING
POCKET BILLIARDS

1

EQUIPPING YOURSELF TO ADVANCE

There's an old saying that it's the man behind the gun, not the weapon, that determines the performance. The same can be said of the man or woman wielding the scalpel or driving the car or swinging the golf club—or stroking a cue.

But equipment *can* make a difference. When you play with anything less than the best, your game is bound to suffer. So, if you can afford it, get yourself the best available cue stick, table, and all the rest. Your investment will pay off in the quality of your game.

CUE STICKS

It's important that you own a cue stick, rather than rely on those available in the billiard parlor. You should always play with a stick that's just right for you in terms of comfort, dimensions, balance, and strength. So try before you buy.

Good cue sticks are available in one- and two-piece models. The two-piece version, with a metal screw at the top of the butt that fits into the bottom of the shaft, is a better bet because it's easier to carry.

Figure on spending at least $100 for your cue stick. If you're aiming at raising the level of your game, you can't expect to get a quality cue stick for much less. And if it's a custom cue you've got your sights on, get ready to part with upwards of $300. I bought one for $600, which I can get more than $1,000 for today. Like good artwork, a good cue appreciates in value.

Smart shoppers aren't taken in by fancy-looking cues. Not only does fancy not always mean good; it can sometimes mean that the adornments added to the stick have weakened its structure. Jeweled decorations won't help your game, anyway.

ADD LENGTH AND WEIGHT

A standard cue stick is 57 inches long, but, as an advanced player, you should select one that's a little longer— 58, 58½, or 59 inches long. There are two basic reasons for the extra length. First, a longer cue is likely to be better balanced because the weight is spread over an extra inch of area. Second, the additional length will give you that much extra reach and keep you from having to use the artificial bridge as often as you would with a shorter cue. As a player who's never been enthusiastic about using the artificial bridge, I consider this the most important advantage of the longer cue. The cue I use is 58¾ inches long.

As far as the weight of the cue is concerned, you'll hear advice about starting with a lighter weight one and working up to a heavier one. My feeling is, however, that you should start out with a fairly heavy one, if you can handle it comfortably. Being a pretty big guy, I use a 21-ounce cue, while a thin player might go with a 20-ounce cue. Most U.S. professional players use a cue that weighs between 20 and 21½ ounces.

Total weight is one consideration; the relative weight of shaft and butt is another. The heavier the shaft, the stronger the wood. Therefore, pros will weigh the shaft to make sure that it weighs approximately 4½ ounces.

You might want to consider shafts of different weight, depending on which game you're using them for. For example, while I use the heavy shaft to play Straight Pool, I use a slightly lighter one for Nine-Ball. The reason I make the change is this: In Straight Pool, you want to work as close as you can to the balls, and I think the heavier shaft keeps the cue ball closer to the object balls. With the heavier shaft, you tend to stay down on the ball and have more control on the cue ball over short distances. In Nine-Ball, on the other hand, there are times when the cue ball has to travel a long distance, and with a lighter (four-ounce) shaft, which doesn't feel as heavy, you tend to be able to maneuver long distances better.

When you use two shafts of different weight, the total weight of the stick will vary because you will always use the same butt. And even if you don't deliberately set out to have shafts of different weight, it's unlikely that you'll be able to get two that match perfectly.

STICK TO GOOD BRANDS

No one made a better cue stick than the late George Balabushka; the ones he fashioned can't be duplicated. But that doesn't mean you can't buy excellent-quality sticks today. Among the better, currently active manufacturers of cue sticks are Gus Szamboti of Philadelphia (who makes the best present-day cues); Dick Helmsteader, who now lives in Japan; Danny James of Josh Cues East; and Bill Stroud of Josh Cues West. While Szamboti specializes in the custom cue business, Helmsteader is basically in the commercial cue line.

MATERIAL EVIDENCE

Whatever the dimensions of the cue stick you choose, buy a wooden one rather than one made of aluminum. The feel of a wooden cue is less affected by changes in temperature than is the feel of a metal cue. Also, while a wooden stick might chip if you hit the table with it (after you've missed an easy shot?), it won't bend in half, as an aluminum one might.

The wood should be as hard and as well dried as possible, cured before it's used, to prevent water from getting into it. A good butt will be made of ebony or something comparable, while a shaft will be made of maple or a similar hardwood.

A shaft won't feel perfectly right—it won't be "true"—until it is seasoned by the oils, dirt, powder, and other substances your hand deposits on it. Once it is thus seasoned, you'll be aware of a big difference in the feel.

To help the process along, you might want to try something I've done successfully with new shafts. Wet the shaft with a washcloth soaked in fairly warm water. When the shaft dries, its pores will be open, so put some lighter fluid

If you buy a two-piece cue stick, be sure the parts fit together correctly and that the screw that connects the pieces isn't off-center.

on a towel or rag and rub the shaft with it to create a sort of bonding or sealing effect. The pores will be filled with an oily substance, leaving the surface smooth and even.

I find lighter fluid more effective than lemon wax or lemon oil, which some pros prefer, and I recommend it for anyone with a cue stick valuable enough to keep in top shape.

Presuming you're buying a two-piece cue, make sure the parts fit together correctly and that the screw is not off-center. The joint of a two-piece cue might swell if it's wet, but for ease of transport, I think a two-piece cue is superior to a one-piece.

GOOD CASE

When you're not using your cue, separate the shaft from the butt and put the pieces in a case, preferably a hard one that will offer good protection if it should be run over or

A good-quality, hard case is a must for storing your cue stick. Be careful when placing the parts in the case. Put the butt in first, straight. When removing the stick, take the shaft or shafts out first.

stepped on. To prevent moisture from seeping in, your case should be lined. Because it is soft and won't scuff the cue parts when they're being removed or placed in the case, fur is an excellent lining material.

The lining should be made from a material that protects the stick from heat, cold, and other elements. Whatever the lining is made of, don't buy a case that's made of vinyl plastic, because, if you hit the side of the table with one of those, you're likely to dent your stick.

You endanger your cue, too, by leaving it where there's a lot of moisture or drastic changes in temperatures, such as in the trunk of your car. And you risk its becoming warped or bent by leaving it up against the wall for days. Obviously, when you're finished using your cue stick you should put it—gently—back into its case.

As with everything else, a quality case costs—from $50 to $500. Among well-constructed cases now on the market are those by Bob Hemple of Fellini Custom Cue Cases, a Texas firm. They're relatively expensive, but because of their excellent construction and use of animal-skin linings, they're worth the price.

A point about using a case: be careful how you place your cue parts in it and how you remove them. Do it carefully, for sure, but also keep these points in mind: The butt should go in—straight—before the shaft goes in. When removing the stick, take the shaft or shafts out first. When removing the butt, take it straight out of the case; otherwise, you risk scratching the wood or wrap.

TIPS ON TIPS

The tip on your cue stick is very important because that's the part of the stick that contacts the cue ball. Without a good, solid tip, you're not going to get the desired feel and a good, solid hit. The tip should be made of leather and have a good, rounded shape, like a half-moon with a nice crown on it. The tip should be between one-eighth and one-quarter inch high and, as far as I'm concerned, very hard—the

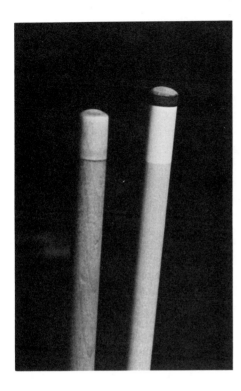

Without a good, solid, rounded tip on your cue stick, you're not going to get a solid hit. The cue at the left has almost no tip left, while the one at the right has a nicely shaped one.

harder the better. A soft tip will flatten out and have you shooting the same way.

Except that the tip should not be hanging over the side of the shaft, you can't really tell by appearances whether or not the tip is a good one. The good-looking one might turn out to be garbage, while the bad-looking one might turn out to be good. There's an element of luck involved in selecting a good tip, which is a very delicate part of your instrument. But you can help make your own luck by dealing with a reputable manufacturer. I prefer tips made by La Professional, a French company.

TREASURY AGENT

Once you've found a good tip, try to keep it in good shape. Besides the practical advantages, a nice, clean tip helps you psychologically, the way a nice, clean nine-iron helps a golfer. As you peer down the shaft, everything looks good.

To help keep cue tips round, smooth, dark, and shiny, pro players periodically rub the side of the tip with a dollar bill (or, bowing to inflation, a ten-dollar bill). The reason we use currency is not to show off or because we're superstitious. Somehow, the chemical agent used in these bills works well on leather cue tips, leaving an attractive finish.

To maintain the rest of the cue, never use sandpaper on the shaft; even the finest grade will wear down the shaft until it's no longer the right diameter. Eventually, if you keep using sandpaper, it will look like a pencil.

Chalk it up to experience.

CHALK TALK

Speaking of chalk, I urge you not to neglect this pool-playing accessory. Chalk that isn't right can cost you a match if it makes you miscue in an important situation. The miscue means you lose your turn, and once your opponent starts shooting, he can go on to win the game. Some wise guys have sabotaged an opponent by wetting his chalk!

Avoid chalk that cakes or falls apart in your hand. I've found that Masters brand chalk seems to adhere to the tip better than any other chalk, and I try to play with this brand all the time. Another good brand is Gandy's National Tournament.

Regardless of the brand you use, be sure to use a new piece when you play, rather than chalk with a deep hole in it, which might result in your getting chalk on the ivory or furl of your cue stick. And you don't want to leave it in a damp place, because even the best-brand chalk will cake if it gets moist.

Beginning players don't always use chalk properly. You should chalk your cue tip before every shot or two, but if you do it incorrectly, you'll defeat the purpose. Hold the

When you chalk your cue stick, it's wrong to move the chalk from side to side. By doing it this way, you don't get an even distribution of chalk, and you get chalk where you don't want it.

The proper way to apply chalk is to hold the chalk steady and, by rolling the stick between your palms and fingertips, rotate the cue.

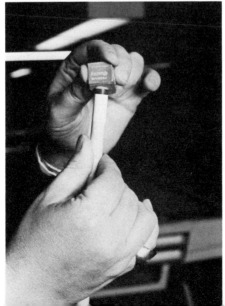

chalk steady and, by rolling the stick between your palm and fingertips, rotate the cue. This ensures an even distribution of chalk all around the tip. Too many players grab the chalk as if it were an orange they wanted to squeeze and rub it around the cue, applying chalk where it doesn't belong. After chalking, examine the tip to make sure the chalk is distributed evenly and fill in any spot you missed with the chalk cube.

Sometimes a tip gets so smooth it won't accept chalk. In that case, you can gently scuff the tip with a file. Be careful, though. If you file with a scraping motion, you might tear the tip. Roll the tip slightly against the file. Then wet the sides of the tip with a damp cloth and, using either the *back* of a piece of sandpaper or a smooth piece of leather, polish the tip. This will harden the sides and keep the tip from extending over the side.

TAKE A POWDER

If your hands sweat a lot, as mine do, you might want to use powder on them. But don't pour it on as if you were treating diaper rash, or you'll get powder where you don't want it, like on your clothing and on the table. Worse, you'll be putting extra oil on your hand, which in turn will make your cue stick very oily. So put powder on sparingly—and only on the part of your hand through which the cue stick slides. And use the least oily powder you can find; most powders specify whether they contain oil.

FURL

On the shaft, right near the cue tip, is a section called *white furl*. Professionals don't like furls made of plastic, so look for a cue with a furl made of ivory or buckhorn. Because of its critical position on the shaft, this area should be treated with care. It can too easily be nicked or scratched.

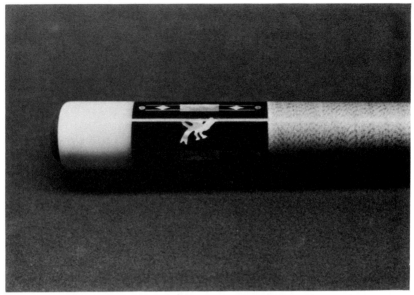

Steve's new trademark is a mythical bird, embossed on the butt of his cue stick.

WRAP

Another part of the stick that should be treated with respect is the wrap—the part of the butt you grasp. If that should get nicked, you'll be aware of an uneven feeling every time you stroke.

Various materials are used for wrapping the cue, but my personal favorite—and the one I recommend—is Irish linen, which absorbs hand sweat much better than leather, nylon, or rubber.

Leather tends to make your hand tacky, yet some good players prefer it because they use a *firm stroke,* in which the hand on the butt doesn't move at all, as compared to a *slip stroke,* in which the hand slides as the player strokes. My hand moves, so that's another reason I prefer the Irish linen.

TABLE TALK

When you're playing in a tournament or in a neighborhood pool parlor you won't have much control over the quality of the table you play on. But you do, of course, when you're looking to buy one for yourself.

Here are some points to consider:

- Don't rule out a *used* table. You have a much better chance of getting your money's worth with a used table than with a used car. A used table that is of good quality and has been kept in good shape will usually need only a change of cloth. An advanced player, who is skilled at controlling the speed of the cue ball, will generally prefer a faster cloth (nylon or a tighter blend of nylon and wool). Others, who have a hard time controlling the cue ball, feel that the slower the cloth (all wool, for example), the better. I have no trouble on either type of cloth, but when I play a less skilled player I'd rather have a fast table because of my opponent's inability to control the ball.

- The better player you are, the better table you want to play on, used or new. For a new table with the quality you want, you can expect to pay $1,000 or better—and that doesn't include the fancy decorative touches that are available.

- Brands make a difference. I'd buy one of these three: Brunswick of Chicago, which makes the best pool table for a commercial establishment; Leisure World of Covina, California, which produces the best table for the home; and Gandy Industries of Macon, Georgia, which offers possibly the best combination of a home and commercial table.

  As with automobiles, each line includes models of varying quality. I have my favorite in each: Brunswick's Gold Crown, Gandy's Big G, and Leisure World's Trafalgar.

  While Brunswick's tables are just about indestructible (when they're taken care of), Gandy's probably won't last as long but are a good buy for the money. Leisure World's are probably the most intricately designed—with such fancy features as carved legs—so they're slightly more expensive than Brunswick's.

- Judging a table needn't be especially complicated. For instance, to find out whether or not it's solid, bump it with your hip. If the table shakes and the balls move or vibrate, you'll know the table is too light and won't hold up. The heavier the table, the better.

  Because every table has its own personality, a pro player will shoot some balls on a table to test it out. He'll stroke a few down the rail and bang a few hard into the side pockets to test them out. Unless you're experienced and know what to look for, though, this won't tell you too much.

- Even though it adds a substantial chunk of cash to your investment, installing a table should be left to some-body who knows his business. This saves you from possible injury and your table from possible damage. Should anything go wrong, such as the slate's cracking, the professional installer is responsible for correcting the problem. He'll also do the extras—attaching the head spot, for example—in a neat, businesslike way.

- Remember, this is furniture that weighs a ton; and, if not installed properly, it can mess up your game perma-nently. For instance, if the table's three slates are not lined up properly, the table is going to have a roll. And one good roll often leads to another.

- Some tables, such as Brunswick's Gold Crown, have leveling devices on the bottom of their legs. If you have a table without such gadgets, all you have to do is slip a matchbook cover or a thin piece of cardboard under the leg that needs to be jacked up.

TABLE DIMENSIONS

Better players prefer to play on larger tables—4½ feet by 9 feet—because the added dimensions give them more room to maneuver the ball, more space for a clear shot. On a smaller table, say 4 by 8 feet, an opponent could score an upset against a superior player, even someone twice as good as he is.

A table smaller that 4 by 8 feet doesn't allow you much room for fun, and if you're serious about improving your game, 4½ by 9 is the size you want.

The size of a pool table's pockets is usually standardized at 5 inches, but some pockets are only 4½ inches. When I had a table with 4½-inch pockets, nobody wanted to play me on it because it was difficult to pocket a ball. When I moved from 4½-inch pockets to 5-inchers, they seemed as big as basketball hoops. As an advanced player, you'll find you'd rather play a lesser opponent on a table with smaller pockets for the simple reason that you're going to make a lot more shots than he will.

PLAYING SURFACE

Earlier I mentioned the speed of the cloth that covers the table surface. As noted, balls move faster or slower depending on the material used. Speed is also affected by how worn the cloth is. As the cloth begins to wear out, the action of the balls may be slowed. You should be prepared to recover your table periodically, say every year or so, depending on how often you use it.

Worn cloth affects your playing in another way. Particularly if the cloth is worn, an older table may have a drift to one side or another, and you'll find the balls "leaning" in that direction. That's one important reason to do what the pros do before competing—check out the table on which the match is going to take place, to become familiar with the feel of the particular table.

As billiard lounges became more family oriented, a trend developed toward more attractive surroundings, and that included a variety of colors for the table cloth. While gold is probably the color that is easiest on the eyes, I'd recommend that you buy a green cloth, because green is the color most commonly in use, and you want to play regularly on the same-color cloth. It will probably hurt your game to own a cloth of a color you'll play on only occasionally.

Most of the tables I recommend are outfitted with True Speed rubber, which I have found to be the best. If the table you buy has rubber that isn't completely satisfactory to you, you can have it replaced.

CARING FOR THE TABLE

A pool table doesn't require a lot of maintenance, provided you don't abuse it and you keep it clean. Some players rap their table for luck (or in anger) with their cue stick; they use it as a whipping—or kicking—boy for their frustrations; they move it or lift it in some demonstration of manliness. All of these are no-nos. Others will let their kids use the pool table as a battleground for their toy soldiers or a playing surface for such other games as table tennis and bowling. This, too, is definitely misuse. Common sense tells you that the pool table should be reserved for the game it's built to accommodate.

Even the best-respected tables will get dirty—from dust in the air, from dye from the chalk on your hand, from pieces of chalk that flake off your cue stick. The more extensively the table is used, the dirtier it gets. What can you do about it? Clean it.

A vacuum cleaner will do the job quickly, but you have to be very careful that it doesn't suck out the plaster of paris that holds the three sections of slate together. If that plaster does come out, it means the ball will be traveling over two grooves the entire width of the table.

The safest implement to use for cleaning the cloth is a brush! Always brush in one direction—toward the rack.

You don't have to do anything about caring for the rubber on the table, because it is covered with cloth. But, because rubber is affected by humidity, try to situate your pool table in a dry area.

The wood on the table's top rail is usually covered with a

material like Formica, which requires only an occasional wiping with a damp cloth. Because the rail covering comes with a highly polished finish that should last a long time, you don't have to concern yourself with polishing the rail.

To protect the table from dust and other substances when you're not playing on it, you might want to keep it covered.

A NEW-BALL GAME

In the so-called good old days, pocket billiard balls were made of clay. Known as *mud balls,* the old-timers were reliable. They didn't make as many erratic spins or rolls as the new ones do.

But progress is progress, and today the game is played with composition balls made of plastic and resin, in about an 80:20 ratio. All of them are a regulation 2¼ inches in diameter with a weight of 5½–6 ounces. The same-size balls would be used on a 4½-by-9-foot, 5-by-10-foot, or 4-by-8-foot table. On anything smaller, where the pockets would be smaller, you'd use balls of 2-inch diameter.

If you do all your playing in a billiard parlor, there's really no need to own your own balls, since they're standardized and most of those you will find in a pool establishment are kept in good condition. But if you have your own table, you will, of course, want to own a set.

The difference in feel we pros experience with different-brand balls may be an entirely imaginary thing, but when you *think* something is different, it might just as well *be* different. So I'm particular about the balls I use. In my opinion, which is shared by most of the championship players, the best balls are Brunswick Centennials, produced by the Albany Billiard Ball Company. Priced now at about $100 per set, they seem to roll and react truer than other brands. In one world tournament a few years ago we were assured that the balls being used (of a different brand) were identical in weight to the Centennials, but they weren't opening on break shots the way we thought they should.

Taking care of billiard balls involves no sweat. Just wash them every once in a while with soap and water and then apply some plastic polish.

If you own, or are a steady customer in, a billiard room, you should make use of a ball-polishing machine, which is expensive but saves a lot of time, effort, and energy and does an excellent job.

MECHANICAL BRIDGE

Mechanical bridges today are made of plastic, as opposed to the mechanical bridges of yesteryear, which had a notched end usually made of metal. When rough, this often prevented a smooth stroke and could nick your cue stick.

I consider the Russo Interlocking Bridge, made by Joe Russo of Trenton, New Jersey, the best bridge manufactured today. His bridges fit together in such a way that you can stack up two, three, or even four of them and shoot over a hill. With the old-style bridges, if you used more than one, there was a good chance one would topple (since they didn't interlock). This, as I learned from bitter experience, could lead you to hit an object ball that wasn't the one you called. The result was a lost turn, and sometimes worse. So buy a few of the interlocking type of mechanical bridge.

A lot of the championship players share my dislike of any type of mechanical bridge and think of it only as a last resort because it's tough to control. Using the longer-than-average cue stick helps you avoid some of the situations in which the mechanical bridge (or *crutch,* as it's sometimes called) would be indicated.

Tip: To do away with the need for a mechanical bridge almost entirely, learn to shoot with the other hand. In other words, if you're right-handed, practice some shots left-handed. This way, you'll be able to manage some shots over balls naturally that used to require the mechanical bridge.

If you do have to rely on the mechanical bridge, be sure that you lay it flat on the table. One sure sign of a beginner

The correct way to use a mechanical bridge is to lay it on the table as flat as possible.

If you lift the mechanical bridge, as so many beginning players tend to do, it's likely to move at the notched end and give you a wobbly, inaccurate stroke.

is lifting its butt. That carries with it the danger that the bridge will wobble, which in turn will make your cue wobble, and you'll end up with an inaccurate shot.

Keep the bridge flat and steady by having the hand that would form your natural bridge hold the mechanical device a few inches from the butt between the middle and index fingers. The heel of the hand should press down firmly on top of the butt of the bridge.

You should keep the bridge on the side of the shot that's away from your shooting hand (to the left, if you're right-handed).

The notched end of the bridge should be just a few inches from the cue ball. Which notch you put your cue through will depend on the way the balls lie and which spot on the cue ball you're aiming for. If you want to shoot over a ball, the high notched part will be up.

To shoot, grip the butt of your cue with a turned-up version of your usual grip. Almost as if you were shooting darts, let the cue rest on your thumb, with your middle and index fingers on top of the stick. With your stroking action coming primarily from the wrist, stroke as if you were throwing a dart with either an overhand or a sidearm motion.

SUMMING UP

To move from beginner to intermediate or advanced player, you should be sure that you're using the best possible equipment—and that includes everything from cue stick to chalk. Obviously, though, no matter how good your equipment, the level of performance you attain is ultimately going to depend on you. Let's discuss how to go about becoming the best possible pool player your talent allows.

2

FINDING YOUR OWN STYLE

When it comes to such fundamentals as stance, grip, and stroke, there are really no absolutes. There's no single correct way to stand or hold the cue stick; essentially, it's the individual's choice. Yet, there are certain general recommendations that should help you, whatever your preferences are.

STANCE

The best way to stand is the way that's comfortable for you. If you're uncomfortable, you're probably going to be off-balance, and you won't be able to hit the ball the way you want to.

But you should place your feet in such a way that your weight is evenly balanced and you won't be knocked over by someone's putting his thumb under your collarbone. (In fact, that's a good way to test your stance.) Also, it usually is a good idea to bend your front knee slightly on most shots.

In an exaggerated pose, Steve shows what a bad stance might look like. With too much tension in the legs, the shooter is off-balance and uncomfortable, and the odds are tremendous against making a good shot.

When you stand the way you're most comfortable, your feet will be apart and parallel, your weight will be evenly balanced, you'll have a good view of your target, and you'll increase your chances of making a good shot.

You probably should stand closer to the table than where the butt of your cue stick is located, and your shooting arm should be able to swing freely, without interference from your body. If you find you're standing so straight that you can't get a good look at the ball or that you're bending over so far that your arm doesn't swing freely, adjust your stance accordingly.

GRIP

Some players like to place their bridge hand only about 6 inches from the cue tip; others prefer it to be as many as 10 inches away. Use the distance that works best for you.

Players also differ a lot in how far from the end they hold the butt of the stick—from way down at the end to pretty far up.

Some keep their butt hand in the same place on the stick throughout their stroke, while others use what is called a *slip stroke,* in which they start at the top of the wrap as they practice-stroke and then slip or slide their power hand back 12 inches to the bottom of the wrap for the actual stroke. (Incidentally, I find that that often is the best stroke for me. But the fact that it works for one player doesn't necessarily mean it will work for you.)

How snugly should you hold the cue butt as you stroke? My only advice is that your grip be neither too tight nor too loose. I grip the butt with three of my fingers, leaving no space between the cue and my hand.

STROKING

The better the player, the more fluid the coordinated action of his wrist, elbow, and shoulder when he strokes. In stroking, your lower arm should swing like a pendulum— and it should be the only part of your arm that moves. Don't swing your upper arm or lift your shoulder.

As you swing, your wrist—which was kept relatively

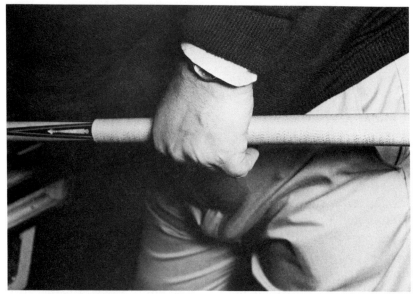

Some players, including Steve, use a slip stroke. They start at the top of the wrap as they practice-stroke . . .

. . . and then slip, or slide, their power hand back 12 inches to the bottom of the wrap for the actual stroke.

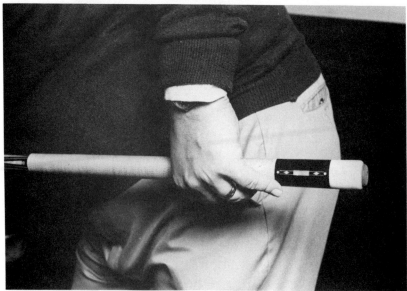

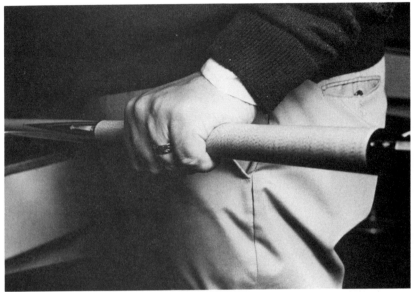

It's a mistake to grip the butt too tightly and to hold it with all five fingers.

The recommended grip is to cradle the butt of your cue in the palm of your hand, with your thumb and index and middle fingers gripping it firmly (but not too tightly) and the other two fingers just along for the ride.

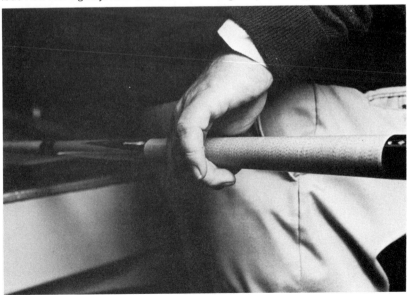

loose and flexible—should whip the cue stick solidly into the cue ball.

Advanced players always remember to take a few practice strokes before *every* shot—whether the shot is easy or tough, short or long. I've seen some excellent players (yours truly included) miss hangers because they didn't take the few seconds to practice-shoot and thus establish a groove for their swing. That failure almost cost me a few thousand dollars in prize money.

The number of practice swings you take should be the same for every shot—not so many that you'll be tired, not so few that you won't have zeroed in on the ball.

Before you stroke, bring your cue stick back by as much distance as there is between your bridge hand and the cue ball. After the shot, follow through so that your cue tip goes *through* the point where the cue ball was. And keep the stick from veering off to one side or another, or the cue ball will do the same. To avoid twisting the cue stick and messing up your shot, keep down in your shooting position

A good stroke . . .

. . . But in a bad follow-through, your cue stick is likely to go flying up into the air, and the cue ball will veer off course.

To avoid twisting your body and spoiling the accuracy of your shot, stay down in position and keep your cue stick on the table as long as possible after making your shot. Good follow-through equals good shooting.

with bridge hand *status quo* and cue stick on the table as long as possible after the shot.

Hit with authority. If you don't stroke with velocity and solidity, if you baby the ball, your cue stick will probably swivel. Don't hit so hard that you lose control, but hard enough that your opponent knows he or she is up against a solid player.

How intense your stroke is will, of course, depend on the situation—a much gentler shot for a one-cushion carom than for a six-cushion. But the speed of the stroke should be uniform, whatever shot you're attempting.

BRIDGES

One of the ongoing controversies in the world of pocket billiards is the relative effectiveness of open and closed bridges. As far as I'm concerned, this is another instance of what works best for you. The late George Chenier, all-time Canadian snooker champion, used an open bridge on every shot, and I saw him run 150-and-out. Canadian and British players tend to prefer open bridges. Others, equally good players, prefer the closed bridge, except in certain special circumstances. If you're asking for advice, I'd say you should pick the bridge you find most comfortable, depending on such factors as how close the cue ball is to the rail and whether or not you have to go over another ball to hit the cue ball.

When possible, it's probably safer to use a closed bridge, because it keeps the cue stick from flying up in the air or going sideways. With an open bridge there's always the danger of losing control. Still, when the cue ball is on the rail you might want to use an open bridge, as you probably would for a follow shot as well.

Your bridge hand should control the shaft of the cue tightly enough that the stick won't wobble, but loosely enough that it moves smoothly when you stroke.

In a closed bridge, don't leave an open space between the pads of your thumb and index finger, because then there's

The closed bridge, with the index finger curled over the cue, is used most often because it prevents the cue stick from going where you don't want it to.

Be careful, though, that you don't leave too much space between the fingers and the cue stick, as shown here, or that you don't grip the stick so tightly that it can't flow smoothly.

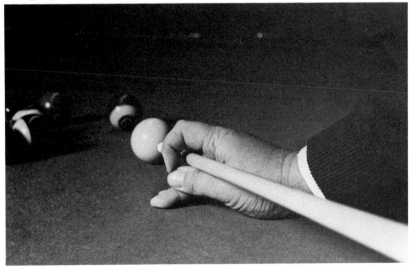

The closed bridge should allow the cue stick to glide smoothly while you keep it under control.

In the open bridge, the cue stick rests on the crease at the base of your thumb, between your thumb and index finger. It's always a matter of preference, but for a **follow shot,** the open bridge is generally recommended.

When the cue ball is close to rail, use a rail bridge, with the rail as your base. There are various types of rail bridges, both open . . .

. . . and closed.

not a proper resting place for the cue. And don't let your index finger overlap your thumb, because the cue will be too unsteady.

You'll know you're grasping the cue too tightly if the skin of your index finger holds back its forward motion.

SHOOTING OVER A BALL

When you shoot over a ball, put your bridge hand as close as possible to that ball without touching the ball with your hand or cue stick. The closer you are to the ball, the truer and more level your stroke will be. Don't stroke until you're sure the bridge is solid, with fingers—from tips to first joints—pressed to the table. Raise the wrist and fingers of your bridge, not the butt of the cue. When shooting over balls, be careful that your stick doesn't hit anything but the cue ball.

When you want to draw a shot, don't raise the butt of the cue, as Steve is demonstrating here. Lower the wrist and fingers of your bridge hand instead.

THE MECHANICAL BRIDGE

You should not stretch for a shot when the situation clearly calls for using the mechanical bridge. As noted earlier, I try to avoid using that crutch under almost all circumstances, but there are times when you must. It's better to have help than to stretch yourself out of position and risk fouling or goofing up your shot.

SPECIAL SHOTS

When a beginner learns to play pocket billiards he is taught to hit high (follow), low (draw), and right- and left-hand English. He is also advised to perfect hitting the cue ball dead center before trying any of these special shots.

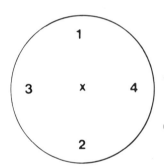

For **follow,** hit cue ball above center (#1).
For **draw,** hit it below center (#2).
To apply **left-hand English,** hit cue ball to left of center (#3).
For **right-hand English,** hit it right of center (#4).

One of the hallmarks of an advanced player is that he not only can use these special shots effectively, but he can use two of them in combination (for example, low right-hand English).

If you've reached that plateau, fine. But be warned: when you use either high or low with a type of English, the ball is going to act differently than if you had used only high or low. If you've hit the cue ball with high right-hand English, when it contacts the object ball the object ball is going to spin to the left. In other words, the object ball will react according to the type of English you applied to the cue ball—and, of course, so will the cue ball (spinning one way as it heads toward the object ball and the opposite way after it makes contact). So you have to make the necessary compensation in your aiming and stroking.

Use English as seldom as possible because you can get into more trouble applying it incorrectly than you can if you don't use it at all. When you must apply English, make your stroke sharp and springy and follow through. And remember to compensate.

BANKS, CAROMS, AND COMBINATIONS

As you become more sophisticated in your pool playing, you'll be trying more complicated shots more often. But select them with the greatest care, because using carom, bank, or combination shots makes it increasingly difficult to make the balls go where you want them to.

CAROMS

There are various types of caroms (or *kisses*, if you prefer). One involves ricocheting the cue ball off one object ball and into another, pocketing the second object ball. Another type involves caroming one object ball off a second to make the first one go into a pocket.

In preparation for this kiss shot, Steve notes that the center of the two object balls is aiming right at the middle of the side pocket.

Often, you'll use a carom—making a ball glance off another—just for the sake of positioning. Sometimes, though, this happens by accident and the balls end up frozen, touching a rail or each other, in a way that causes you trouble.

BANK

A bank shot involves driving the object ball into one or more cushions on its way to the pocket. You have to keep in mind that, as the speed of the ball increases, the angle of the bank shot increases.

A straight-in shot is always easier. You can bank on that.

COMBINATIONS

A combination shot involves driving the cue ball into one or more object balls, which in turn strike the object ball you're trying to sink. Unless the combination is lined up

Before trying a combination shot, line up the two object balls. Then pick out the point to hit on the first ball so that it drives the second into the hole.

absolutely straight for the hole, you're better off taking a different shot. If you must try the combination, concentrate closely on the ball immediately before the one you're trying to pocket; that's the one that will tell you whether the angle is proper for making the shot.

Mission accomplished! Steve has hit the first ball in such a way that it has propelled the second toward the side pocket.

POSITION

As an advanced player, your philosophy about position play will vary, depending on which game you're playing.

For example, an important element in success in Straight Pool is knowing what you're going to do with the last five balls on the table—in what order you intend to sink them and in which pockets.

Novices tend to approach the situation with a sink-them-all-or-nothing attitude; more experienced players will try to leave themselves a safety valve, an "out" in case they get into trouble and find themselves confronting a shot that doesn't look right.

Playing position in Nine-Ball does not allow you as much flexibility, because balls have to be pocketed in numerical order. So there are few alternatives as far as position is concerned. Better players will not have to be reminded that the less distance the cue ball has to travel, the better off they are.

In Eight-Ball you have to be very careful, if you're not

A good drill for practicing position is putting the object balls into an "L" formation, and pocketing each one, starting with the ball closest to the rail.

Another good position drill is to arrange object balls in a circle, with the cue ball in the middle. Try to pocket each ball while making sure the cue ball touches only the specific object ball and does not touch a rail.

sure of running out, that you don't leave your opponent and his or her object balls with the cue ball at one end of the table. Because then your opponent is likely to run out. If chances are great that the other player is going to have his or her balls free and clear, play safe.

The whole emphasis in One-Pocket is on snookering your opponent. Try to lag a ball by your pocket and snooker him behind another ball so that he can't get that ball away from his pocket.

A perfect safe in One-Pocket. Because the other object balls have snookered the cue ball, your opponent can't hit that lone object ball that's near the pocket.

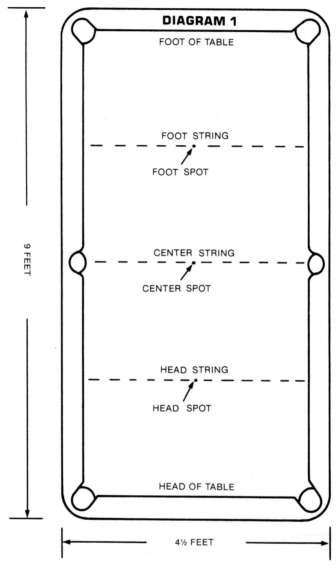

Overhead view of the pocket billiards table, showing the pockets and spots.

3

GAME PLANS

This may be old news to many of you, but it doesn't hurt to go over the basics of the main games played at a pool table. You may have forgotten some of the rules, and there may be a couple you never even knew.

14.1 CONTINUOUS POCKET BILLIARDS

The granddaddy of them all—in the sense that, once you master it, you can play all the rest—is 14.1 Continuous Pocket Billiards, also known as *Straight Pool* and *Call Shot*.

It's called *continuous* because once 14 of the 15 object balls have been pocketed, the game continues with the racking up of those pocketed balls. It's sometimes referred to as *call shot* because the shooters must call their shots— that is, announce the ball they're aiming at and the particular pocket they are trying to drop it into.

As you probably know, you get one point for each designated ball you hit into a designated pocket. You also get a point for any ball that is pocketed along with the ball you called.

Games are won by the first player to reach a certain number of points, say 50 or 75, decided on by you and your opponent or by the rules committee of a tournament before games begin. Major tournament games are usually 150-point contests.

FOR STARTERS

In any game played on a pool table the *opening break* is one of the most important shots. This is the shot in which the racked-up balls are broken apart. And, because pool is one game that can be won before the winner's opponent has a chance to play, it's no simple pun that the opening break can make or break your game.

But, unlike some of the other major games played on a pool table, 14.1 is a competition in which it's an advantage *not* to break. That's because it's so hard to make a called shot on the break, and there's a good chance you might leave your opponent with easy shots.

To decide which of you has the dubious distinction of breaking in 14.1, you can choose by selecting either odds or evens and putting out one or two fingers at a given count, or you can flip a coin, or you can lag, which is what the pros do. In lagging, you each take a turn shooting the cue ball down to the foot rail so that it comes back as close to the head rail as possible. The player whose ball ends up closer to the head rail has the option of whether or not to break.

A lot of players forget that winning the toss or lag gives them the choice of breaking or requesting that their opponent do it. Veteran pool followers still tell about a balkline carom championship in which both competitors wanted their opponent to break and mistakenly tried to lose the lag on purpose. The fellow who did break (Jake Schaefer, Jr.), because he had accidentally won the lag, went on to run a record 400 for the title. His opponent (Erich Lagenlacher) never got a chance to shoot. It's amazing that neither of the two men vying for a world title remembered that the winner of the lag had the option of shooting first or requesting that his opponent take the opening shot.

Once it is determined who is to shoot the opening break (in straight pool), the 15 numbered object balls are racked up in a triangle with the ball at the head of the triangle on the foot spot.

The shooter has the cue ball in hand, meaning he can place it anywhere between the head string and the head of the table. The particular game and your strategy will determine where you should place your cue ball, as well as how much force you should use on your stroke, the spot you should try to hit on the cue ball, and where in the rack of balls you should aim the cue ball.

Keep in mind that, in 14.1, you'll *scratch*—and be minus two points—unless on the opening break you drive the cue ball and two or more of the object balls to a cushion. So this, too, will affect where you place the cue ball. You'll be influenced further by a main objective of the opening break shot: leaving your opponent with either no shot or a very difficult one.

I generally place the cue ball on the head string, to the right of the head spot. Then, using right-hand English, I try to clip about a quarter of the ball that's in the rear right-hand corner of the triangle. Stroking the cue ball just to the right of the middle gives it the right-hand English that will make the cue ball brush off the object ball, then bounce off the rear cushion at one of the diamonds, hit a side rail at a diamond near the foot of the table, and then hit a diamond on the opposite side of the table.

Because the chance of making a called shot on the opening break is so slim, you probably won't even bother making a call (though there's nothing lost if you do). Should a ball go into a pocket, when either ball or pocket wasn't the designated one, the ball is *spotted* (placed) on the foot spot or, if that's occupied, placed directly behind the ball that's already on the foot spot. The imaginary line from the foot spot to the middle of the foot of the table is called the *long string*.

Steve racks the balls for 14.1 opening break.

Note where the cue ball is placed for opening break in 14.1—in line with the head spot and with the second diamond on the head rail.

In good opening break in 14.1, cue ball hits just about one-quarter of the ball at the rear right corner of the rack.

Steve looks over the aftermath of his good opening break in 14.1. The cue ball is frozen to the head rail, and his opponent has no shot.

If you don't pocket the ball you called in a pocket you designated, you lose your turn.

You will lose a point as well if the cue ball scratches by going into a pocket (whether or not an uncalled object ball is pocketed at the same time). Should the ball you called go into the pocket you designated on the same shot that the cue ball is pocketed, the point you would have received is nullified. Otherwise, a point is subtracted when the cue ball is pocketed.

When this happens, an object ball is taken out and placed on the foot spot (or right behind a ball that is already there). Your opponent may place the cue ball anywhere behind the head string.

OTHER SCRATCHES

There are several other ways to scratch besides pocketing a cue ball or failing to pocket an object ball or contact a cushion along with at least two object balls on the opening break.

You scratch and lose a point if the cue ball jumps off the table. In most competitions, if an object ball should jump off the table, it will be spotted at the foot string without loss of a point, though your turn would end, as it does with any scratch. In championship play, however, an object ball that goes off the table will also cost you a point.

If, accidentally or deliberately, you cause the cue ball to jump up by elevating the butt end of the cue stick and striking the cue ball in the center or above center, it's a legal jump. But if you dig under the cue ball with the tip of your cue stick, making the ball jump, you may lose a point.

You also scratch anytime your cue ball fails to hit another ball or if both your cue ball and an object ball fail to hit a rail, unless a ball is pocketed.

To prevent your cue ball from following an object ball into the pocket, use *draw;* in other words, hit the cue below center to make the cue ball stop or come back. Or, if you hit it dead center, either don't hit it hard or hit it in such a way that it glances off the object ball at a slight angle. You might aim to hit the object ball a little to one side. If not, use draw to make the cue ball come back. Obviously, when the object ball is at an angle between cue ball and pocket, you'll hit the cue ball off to the side that's away from the pocket.

SCRATCHING WITH A PURPOSE

There's so much emphasis on how to avoid scratching that players sometimes don't realize there are occasions when they should scratch deliberately. This is done rather than risking setting up an opponent for a long run on an open table. It's an integral part of defensive play that good competitors employ.

In 14.1 Continuous, every scratch, whether or not it is deliberate, costs you a point. If you scratch three shots in a row, you're assessed an extra 15 points on top of the point per scratch. Believe it or not, there are times when good players elect to lose those 18 points—sometimes starting out in the game with a score of −18—rather than risk letting their opponent get off on a tremendous run.

For example, you might be better off taking one scratch (or more) than opening the game with a break that scatters the balls all over the table and gives your opponent shots that are wide open. Or you might be up against a tough shot, say a cluster of balls, that you're not confident of making. So you decide to take your penalty and let your opponent break open the cluster.

Outside of championship-level play, though, you're probably wise never to scratch deliberately more than twice in a row. For the average player, that extra 15-point penalty is too great a burden. And, as if those extra 15 points aren't enough of a handicap, you're then forced to break open all 15 balls, as you would at the beginning of the game.

Deliberate scratching is one aspect of playing safe. But there are some other elements to watch out for in this regard. For instance, when you *play safety* with an object ball that is frozen against a cushion, you stand to lose a point unless you pocket the object ball, make the cue ball contact a cushion after it strikes the object ball, or drive the object ball to another cushion.

Even if you don't violate this rule, you're allowed to play safety in this situation only twice in a row. On the third shot you must either drive the object to a different rail or drive the cue ball to any rail after it makes contact with the object ball. If you fail to do one or the other, all 15 balls will be racked and you'll have to break, just as you would to open the game.

Another fine point to remember is that, when the cue ball is touching an object ball and you play directly at that object ball, you have to move the object ball and make the cue ball hit a cushion or you have to drive that object ball to a cushion. If you don't do one of these things, you lose a point and your turn.

KEY BALL/BREAK BALL

As I mentioned, what makes the game of 14.1 continuous is the fact that, after 14 of the object balls have been pocketed, the 15th ball stays on the table as the *break ball,* the 14 pocketed balls are racked up, and the game continues.

Your chances of running up a high score or *running out*— winning the game—depend on how well you handle the transition from when only one or two balls are left on the table to when they're reracked and all 15 are back in play. A key to your progress is how well you handle the *key ball,* the next-to-last ball on the table before the balls are reracked.

A good player decides, when several balls are left, which will be the key shot and which the break shot. If you can make the right decision, pocket the key ball, and get into good position for the break shot, you're progressing very well as a player.

The ball you select as the break ball should be fairly close to where the rack of balls will be placed. Standard strategy is to sink the break ball in a pocket you designate and then make the cue ball carom off the break ball into the rack of balls. It's all right, too, if the cue ball caroms from the break ball into one or more cushions and then into the rack.

Contrary to what some players believe, you are *not required* to shoot at the break ball. When the 14 other balls are reracked, any one of them is fair game, and you continue shooting until you miss or scratch or until you accumulate enough points to win the game. But a word of caution: if you choose to shoot into the rack rather than at the break ball, you must pocket a ball, drive an object ball to a cushion, or make the cue ball hit a cushion after it contacts an object ball.

Incidentally, if the last ball on the table is lying within the perimeter of the triangle where the other balls are going to be reracked, that break ball is spotted on the head spot. If the cue ball *and* the break ball interfere with the racking of the 14 balls, all 15 object balls are reracked. When the cue ball interferes with the racking of the balls, one of two things occurs:

- If the break ball is outside the head string, you get the cue ball in hand and can place it anywhere behind the head string for the break.
- If the break ball is within the head string and the head of the table, the cue ball is placed on the head spot. (Should the break ball happen to be there, it is moved to the center spot, so the cue ball can be placed on the head spot.)

NINE-BALL

One of the favorite betting games of pool players, especially hustlers, is Nine-Ball, which is a relatively short game. (Not always, though. It once took me six hours to lose $2,500 to a friend in a Nine-Ball match. We made the competition Five-Ahead, which meant the player who led his opponent by five games won the purse. Several times I managed to get four ahead but then faltered and ended up losing it all.) Hundreds, even thousands, of dollars can change hands in just a few minutes. But, whether you bet on it or not, it's a fun kind of game.

The object of the game is simple—sink the 9-ball in accordance with the rules—but competition often is complicated, and luck plays a very important role.

To start the game, object balls 1–9 are racked at the foot spot in diamond shape. The 9-ball is in the middle of the rack, the 1-ball is at the head of the formation. The other balls are placed at random within the diamond.

This is one game in which the player who breaks has the advantage, since it's quite possible he might make a ball and continue sinking balls until he runs out. Conceivably, he could even make the 9-ball on the break!

When I break in Nine-Ball I place the cue ball only about two or three inches to the right of the head spot. I aim my cue stick at the center of the cue ball, trying to drive it right at the middle of the 1-ball as hard as I can.

The strategy on the break is to break the balls wide open and sink any one of them. (If you sink the 9-ball, the game is over, with you the winner.) If you were to pocket the 3-ball, for example, you would then begin with the 1-ball and

When balls are racked for Nine-Ball, the 9-ball should be in the middle of the diamond, and the 1-ball on the head spot. The other object balls are placed at random in the diamond.

try to sink the remaining balls in numerical order, until you
pocket the 9-ball.

It's legal to play a combination involving the 9-ball just as
long as you also hit the ball you're aiming at—the one that's
next in succession. If you hit the 1-ball, and that hits the 9-
ball, and they both go in, you win the game right then.

You don't have to call your shots, but you do have to be
careful of scratching. Pocketing the cue ball used to mean
only that your turn was ended and your opponent got the
cue ball in hand between the head string and the head of the
table. But in recent years a new rule was introduced for
Nine-Ball tournaments (as well as for Eight-Ball and Seven-
Ball) that raised players' blood pressure and spectators'
interest.

The new rule provided that anytime after the break, if you
pocket the cue ball or fail to hit the object ball you're aiming
at, you not only lose your turn, but your opponent gets the
cue ball in hand *anywhere on the table!* This is obviously a
tremendous advantage that should just about guarantee an
accomplished player the game. (If you scratch in the pocket
on the break, your opponent still gets the cue ball behind the
head string.)

The rule, which was enacted to please TV viewers, encour-
ages safeties and slows the game somewhat. But it's still an
interesting, relatively fast-paced competition.

The importance of the break in Nine-Ball can't be overem-
phasized. If you make a ball on the break, you have a good
chance of winning the game before your opponent gets a
chance to shoot. Once, in a four-handed series of Nine-Ball,
in which turns were determined by lot, I didn't get a chance
to shoot for 12 games! When I finally got a shot it wasn't a
good one, and I went another 12 games without an opportunity to shoot.

On the break, hit the cue ball with a good, solid stroke,
contacting it about a tip above center. Drive it directly at the
center of the front ball in the rack. But beware of letting the
cue ball run amok and land in a pocket. I once saw a player
involved in a 21-game session (the winner is the first to take

11 games) who won the break and scratched five times in a row. Costly? There was $2,000 on the line.

In a friendly game of Nine-Ball you can elect to play one of two versions: *Hit-the-Ball* or *One-Shot Shootout.*

The basic difference shows up when the ball you want to hit is *snookered* behind another ball, making a straight-in shot impossible. In Hit-the-Ball you must make an honest attempt at the shot. In One-Shot you can stroke the cue ball so it doesn't hit anything, without being penalized.

In One-Shot, therefore, you might try to hit the cue ball to a part of the table that leaves your opponent with a very difficult shot. Your opponent then has the option of trying to make that difficult shot or declaring that he wants you to attempt it. If he designates you to try, and you miss the ball this time, he gets the cue ball in hand anywhere he wants it. If, however, he decides to take that tough shot and misses, then *you* get the cue ball in hand anywhere on the table.

There's no limit on how many times a player can hit the cue ball to leave his opponent with a hard shot, without hitting an object ball, provided he doesn't do it on two shots in succession.

Hit-the-Ball is more exciting because you never know where the balls will end up, so smaller bettors tend to prefer that version. Big bettors seem to like One-Shot Shootout.

Nine-Ball can be played with up to five competitors. The game played by four or five at a time is sometimes known as *Ring Nine-Ball,* a game in which the luck of the draw is almost as important as your performance. If you draw fourth or fifth, you may not get a chance for a dozen games.

Because Nine-Ball is over much more quickly than 14.1, it's a favorite of hustlers, who pretend to be rotten players until the ante is high enough for their liking. So be on the alert.

ONE-POCKET

For this game, you and your opponent each select a pocket before the game begins. Only balls sunk in your pocket will count for you; only those sunk in his will count for him.

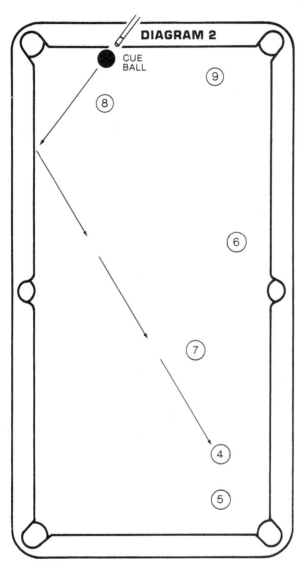

Having made the 3-ball in this Nine-Ball game, you failed to get good position for the 4-ball and wound up behind the 8-ball. This means you have to kick at the 4-ball—carom the cue ball off the rail at the 4-ball. If you fail, your opponent gets the cue ball in hand. If you can sink the 4-ball and get position on the 5-ball, you'll probably run out. So practice hitting the ball off the rail for situations like these.

The object of the game is to pocket eight of the object balls in your pocket before your opponent gets eight in his or hers.

In almost every instance the pocket you each select will be at the foot of the table. The reason? That's where balls are likely to go on the break.

All 15 object balls are racked in the triangle at random. They do not have to be pocketed in rotation, and you don't have to call the ball you're trying to pocket. You would probably lag for break.

One-Pocket is a game that's often compared with chess because you have to think four or five moves ahead. Your emphasis should be on defense—making shots that leave your opponent with the hardest possible bank. This is a game in which the one who takes gambles generally loses.

If you end up having to break, hit what is known as a *safe break,* a very easy hit to protect yourself. Try to get as many balls as possible near your pocket without leaving your opponent with a clear shot at his or hers. Your opponent will have to get the balls that are near your pocket away; if not, you'll probably go on to sink two, three, or more.

A good way to hit a safe break is to split the first two balls at the top of the triangle.

An important part of playing One-Shot well is the carom or bank shot because, chances are, your opponent isn't going to leave you with any straight-on shots. But these are extremely difficult and shouldn't really be tried until you've mastered the straight shots.

EIGHT-BALL

This is the game that gave us the expression "winding up behind the 8-ball." And no wonder. That's essentially a hopeless predicament, and this game is loaded with them. In fact, Eight-Ball is a game in which so much can go wrong that you have to try as hard as you can not to lose the game as you try to do things to win it.

The object of the game is to pocket a specific 7 of the 15

object balls and then pocket the 8-ball before your opponent sinks his or her 7 object balls and then the 8-ball. One player (or team) has to pocket the balls numbered 1–7; the other, those numbered 9–15. The 8-ball must be saved for last.

Which group of balls is yours is determined after the break, in which all 15 balls are racked up at the foot spot in triangular shape, with the 8-ball in the middle.

If you break, you should drive the cue ball as hard as you can to sink whatever balls you can. If you manage to sink one or more balls on the break, you have your choice of either the group numbered 1–7 or the group numbered 9–15. Your opponent is then assigned the other category of balls. If you don't pocket any balls on the break, your opponent gets the choice.

Should you pocket one ball on the break, it makes sense to choose the category to which that ball belongs. If you've sunk two balls from one group and one ball from the other, then pick the group to which the two belong. If you sink one from each group, the choice is arbitrary, though you should probably consider the position of the remaining balls in making your selection.

If you should pocket the 8-ball on the opening break, you automatically win the game.

If your opponent breaks and fails to sink any balls, determine which category has the most balls within easy-shot range of a pocket and choose that category as yours.

The only shot you have to call is the one involving the 8-ball—after you've sunk your required seven.

You get credit for every ball you pocket legally. Should you accidentally sink a ball that's within your competitor's group of balls, he or she gets credit for it and your turn ends. If you sink one of your balls and one of your opponent's at the same time, your turn continues, but your opponent still gets credit for his or her ball.

Now for all the bad news—some of the many ways you can lose the game:

• Let's say you've pocketed all seven balls in your category and are now ready to try for the 8-ball. You have to call the pocket you're aiming for, and, should the 8-ball go into a pocket other than the one you've called, you lose the game.

- You also lose if, when shooting directly at the 8-ball without banking, you don't do one of three things: pocket the 8-ball, make it hit a cushion, or have the cue ball hit a cushion after striking the 8-ball.
- If, except on the break, you pocket the 8-ball before the seven object balls in your group, guess what? You lose.
- If you're banking for the 8-ball, you have to hit it or lose the game.
- When you're playing for the 8-ball you have to hit that ball first. You'd lose the game if you pocketed it on a combination.
- When you're shooting to make the 8-ball, if the cue ball scratches in a pocket, you lose the game.

If you haven't given up on the game before you started playing it, there are some other pointers to keep in mind.

For example, when you have cue ball in hand and there are object balls within the head string, place the object ball that's nearest to the string on the foot spot. You do the same thing when the 8-ball is the object ball and is lying within the head string and you have the cue ball in hand.

Rules can vary tremendously in Eight-Ball, and you and your opponent can modify them to your liking. Some people play that, if the 8-ball goes in on the break, the breaker doesn't win; the balls are just reracked, and the game starts again.

If you want to make this already difficult game even tougher, you can decide you have to pocket the 1-ball in the right side pocket as you face the foot of the table. If you have the high-numbered balls, you have to put the 15-ball in the left side pocket. If these balls aren't dropped into designated pockets, they're respotted until they are.

Combination shots are permitted except when you're trying to sink the 8-ball.

Sound like fun?

4

YOU'RE NEVER TOO GOOD TO LEARN

I've always believed that you can learn by watching good players and then incorporating elements of their game into your own. The players you watch needn't be professionals, though you can't find much better examples. Observe players of your own caliber or slightly better and then experiment with whatever it is that looks good in their game and seems to be an improvement over yours.

It may be only one item that you adapt—say the other fellow's approach to positioning or where he places the cue ball for the opening break—but that one little thing you learn might help you win five matches.

When I was starting out I always watched the good players and then tried out what I saw them doing. Even as I've become more successful and experienced, I still find the examples of others helpful. I play against Allen Hopkins a lot, and we learn from each other—how to go around balls, for example, and all sorts of other things. He may currently be the best One-Pocket player in the country, so what I'm likely to pick up from him is a tip related to that game, which is really a game of chess. And he probably picks up some of my Straight Pool technique. You're never too good to learn.

The thing to remember is to give a fair chance to what you're trying to incorporate into your game from other players. It's not going to fit into your style just like that. And if you find that you admire the playing style of two good players, whose styles are very different from each other's, give each a reasonable trial period and then settle on the one that fits you more comfortably. Above all, keep your eyes and mind open to different ideas you can pick up from other players, including your archrival.

PRACTICE

For years I've been preaching that the best way to practice is to play against someone. To get the necessary competitive edge you have to be competing—and not just against yourself. This advice applies more to better players than to beginners, because beginners are still working on things they can improve, while advanced players have mastered all the fundamentals and are using their practice time just to fine-tune their game.

For advanced players, just going to the pool room, picking up a cue stick, and starting to practice might be a waste of time. In fact, it could even be counterproductive. For example, they might get bored and lose concentration and end up missing shots they'd normally make with ease. Disgusted with their performance, they might then decide to go to the movies or go home and watch TV. To be able to play this game, you have to be in the right frame of mind, so practice in a way that means something.

An old pro, the late Onofrio Laurie, used to advise against overpracticing because it tends to make you stale. I've abided by that advice for years. In the half-hour or so before a match I'll practice—but for the purpose of warming up and getting loose, rather than trying to make last-minute improvements in my game.

HIT WITH AUTHORITY

As an advancing player, you'll want to hit the ball a little bit harder than you did as a beginner. You don't have to watch a good player to know he or she is advanced; hearing is enough. Close your eyes, and the "whack, whack, whack" sound as the pro pockets one ball after another will tell you that the player is hitting with authority.

You should try to do the same, because more balls are missed when you hit easily or somewhere between easily and hard than are missed when you hit hard. When you ease up on your stroke it's as if you're trying to do something besides just making the ball, and that's when you tend to miss.

KNOW THE SCORE

It's more than an expression to say you should always know the score. For how close or wide the margin is will often determine how you play.

For example, suppose you're playing Straight Pool to 100, and you're ahead by 95–20. You may tend to be a defensive player, but with that large a lead, you can afford to take a chance with a difficult shot and try to end the game. Otherwise, if you keep playing safe until you have a clear-cut shot, your opponent may peck away at your lead with runs of 20 and 30 and go on to win. He or she might even do it in one turn, with a run of 80, while you sit there helpless. With a 75-point lead, you should try to end the game in a hurry.

The same advice applies in Nine-Ball, when you need one game to win the session, while your opponent needs five. Say you've got what shapes up as an impossible shot—the 1-ball and 9-ball are close together—and you don't think you'll be able to run out. Well, it doesn't hurt to ride that 9-ball a little bit; with luck, it may get into a pocket.

When I played Allen Hopkins in the final of a tournament in Virginia and the score was 10–10, he broke. The cue ball jumped off the table, and the 9 and the 1 were left in a screwy combination setup. The other balls were all tied up, and I knew I wouldn't be able to run out. I decided to gamble and take a chance riding the 9. I made a nice combination and won the match and the tournament. That was one time when gambling on a shot paid off. But you have to weigh each situation carefully.

KNOW YOUR OPPONENT

Just as you should always know the score, you should always know your opponent, if you're going to be able to control the game. You must not let him control you.

Suppose, for example, your opponent is a slow, methodical player, who looks over any kind of shot for three minutes before stroking. He's going to make you fall asleep in your chair. But that's not the worst of it (the nap might do you good); the danger is that you're liable to start copying your opponent's pace, which means you'd be playing his or her style, not your own. The important thing is to play your own game.

There's a more positive side to knowing your opponent, though. If you were playing someone with the style of Irving Crane, who's a super defensive player, you would try to leave him long, difficult shots to make, because, although he's one of the best around the ball for position and for safety play, he is not a long, difficult shot maker. So you want to keep him as far away from the ball as possible.

On the other hand, if you're playing an offensive player, a Lou Butera, for example, who shoots at everything, you shouldn't mind leaving him close to the ball. He'd rather find a shot than play safe. As a player who shoots at everything and anything, sometimes he makes a shot and sometimes he misses.

Classifying your opponent as either a defensive or an offensive player is very helpful in Nine-Ball, One-Pocket, and Straight Pool; it's also of some value in Eight-Ball, though considerably less than in the other games.

It's always helpful to know in which game an opponent excels and in which he's just so-so. Being good at one game on a pool table doesn't guarantee being good at another.

A good illustration is that of Allen Hopkins, who, I think, is the finest One-Pocket player in the country but isn't tops in Nine-Ball or Straight Pool. He practices and plays a lot of One-Pocket, which is no surprise since a lot of people like to concentrate on what they do best. This sets a cycle in motion: you play more of what you're good at, so you become even better at it, and so on. Allen's also better equipped mentally for One-Pocket than for other games.

Similarly, a road player named Grady Matthews is an excellent Nine-Ball and One-Pocket player, but he can't spell Straight Pool.

Jimmy Fusco is a great One-Pocket player, a good Nine-Ball player, and a horrible Straight Pool player. His head isn't right for that game.

What accounts for the differences in these and other players is that in Straight Pool you have to think very far ahead, while in Nine-Ball and One-Pocket you're thinking of the current game and getting from the 1-ball to the 2 and then to the 3, and so forth.

The biggest fault a good player is guilty of in One-Pocket is taking a lot of chances. The reason Allen Hopkins is so good at the game is that he takes almost *no* chances. He's slow, deliberate, and patient—all perfect qualities for a One-Pocket player.

Some people feel your best defense is a good offense, but I like Hopkins's style of play better than mine for One-Pocket. In other words, this is one game where a good defense will overcome a good offense. The rare times Allen takes a gamble are usually the times he makes mistakes in this game; it's when I try to play safe that I make mistakes.

In Straight Pool, though, I'm convinced that under present-day conditions, the good offensive player should beat the good defensive one. The more balls you pocket, the more points you get, and you consequently win the game. Obviously, you pocket the balls by shooting them in the holes, not by playing safe or trying to snooker the other guy. If your offense is in gear, that will be all the safeguard you need.

Let me put it another way: if Irving Crane and I played Straight Pool in a game that restricted us to a run of 28 and then required us to play safe, I would like his chances better than mine to win the game. But games aren't played with any such restrictions, so I'd like my chances to win better than his. I can get up and run 80 or 100, while he likes to get up and hit you with, say, 42, and then play safe.

The best type of player for Nine-Ball is a mixture of the better Straight Pool type and the One-Pocket type. You have to possess the mental sharpness that lets you know when and when not to take a gamble. Missed chances in this game are especially costly; if you shoot and miss, nine chances out of ten, you'll lose.

Still, while the key to this game is pocketing the ball, a good offensive player should beat a good defensive player. Case in point: Mike Sigel of Baltimore, whose offense is extremely powerful and who may be the best Nine-Ball player around today. His defense is questionable, but his offense is so effective that he seldom has to play defensively. Ideally, though, a Nine-Ball player should combine good offense with good defense.

In Eight-Ball it's difficult to say whether a defensive or an offensive player has the edge. The dangerous opponent is the one who can execute better, who can put his or her cue ball in a certain spot to open two balls. But this is a game in which a lesser player, by running only seven balls and then pocketing the 8, can beat a better player. The better player may never get to the table. And, because luck plays such an important part, it's hard to classify the player likely to win.

Knowing which game your opponent is better at is essential to your chances of winning—a game or a bet. You don't handicap a player in a game at which you know he or she excels; in fact, if you can help it, you don't play that person in that game.

STICK TO YOUR GAME

Professional pool players do not have a game plan *per se,* because there are too many variables. You can't really anticipate what's going to happen out there. So what you do is use the basic general strategy that best suits you.

What best suits me is offense, while what best suits a player like Irving Crane is defense. A player who favors defense would rather play on a table that is 5 feet by 10 feet, which were the dimensions of the tables years ago. As an offensive player, I'd rather play Irving on a table that is 4½ by 9.

Whatever type of game you favor, you should stick to your game—whatever happens. Even if your opponent is leading you by a score of 80-10, you'll be better off adhering to your basic style of play. Of course, amateurs or novice players have enough difficulty making the ball in the pocket and (possibly) getting into good position for the next ball, so they may not even realize what their playing style is. But the better player, which you're striving to be, will know the style that suits him or her best and will stay with it through thick and thin.

KEEP COOL!

A basic problem that keeps a lot of players—amateurs and pros alike—from realizing their full potential as players is that they come into a game *uptight.* Sometimes it's the result of an argument with spouse or girlfriend or boy-friend, neighbor or brother; sometimes, it's the outgrowth of concern about health or bankbook. But usually it's the game itself that causes a lot of players to be uptight. And the more important the game or the tournament, the more tense they become.

In any sport—and, for that matter, in most aspects of life—you can't do your best if you're so somber, solemn, and straitlaced that you feel hemmed in. You've got to learn to relax.

"Easier said than done," you reply—and you're absolutely right. Learning to control your anxiety and relax has to come from within yourself. You can't learn it, but you can practice it. One approach is to try to copy athletes who seem to have mastered tension. What does someone like golfer Lee Trevino do? To relax, he jokes with other players and spectators, gets into some witty repartee with them, and before you know it, he's as laid-back as a guy in a hammock on a summer afternoon.

In that respect I'm a Lee Trevino type. I like to joke and clown around and talk to people. I even talk to myself sometimes. You can't hold things in too long, or you'll bust. In some of the U.S. Opens and other major tournaments that I've won I've managed to joke around even when I was running behind. That's just a method to relax myself that I've found successful.

This is not to suggest that I don't take the game seriously; beneath my joking exterior is a solid interior just hungering to eat up the balls and put them in the pocket. A case in point was the 1983 Spring Open played in New York City.

I was playing Allen Hopkins in Nine-Ball, and I had him, 4-0, going for 11. Then he caught me at 4 and went ahead, either 8-4 or 9-4. Though I was trailing, I kept joking with some fans in order to keep calm. I managed to relax and then fought back and won.

Try to find your own gimmicks to help you relax, even if they're superstitions. There are players who wear favorite clothes when they play—for instance, white socks, even with a tuxedo. Richard Riggie, a very good player, used to do that with a flourish. Not only were his socks white, but they were pushed down to his ankles with a rubber band around each sock.

The late Onofrio Laurie used to walk around the table whistling to himself as a way of keeping calm. Arthur Cranfield lays out chalk cubes on all the diamonds along the rails of the table before he shoots, and I constantly rub the

Steve is pleased with the predicament he's put his opponent in.

tip of my cue stick with a dollar bill or even sandpaper. (Though I do it on the tip, I must emphasize that no one should use sandpaper anywhere on the shaft.) I also find that powdering my hands before a match has a calming effect. A prematch back rub can be very soothing, for nerves as well as spine.

Back in their rooms, some players may read or watch TV

Forgive him if he gloats a little.

or just rest with their eyes closed, to relax before competition. Some others deliberately avoid doing anything that may strain their eyesight.

ONE-SIDED CONTESTS

Being far behind or far ahead leads to other potential mental problems, unless you steel yourself against them.

But if the situation is reversed—and Steve is the one who has to shoot—it's a much different expression he wears.

When You're Far Behind

Don't Give Up. Many a player trailing an opponent who needs just one ball or one game to win concedes the competition and stops trying. That's a serious mental error. True, most times the player with the big lead will end up winning, but not always. As Yogi Berra supposedly said about baseball: "The game's not over 'til it's over."

"Phew, this game is tough."

That lesson has been driven home to me time and time again. I'll never forget a match I had in the Michigan Open several years back. I was playing Dick Lane in Straight Pool to 125 points, and he had me by a score of 121 to minus 19! He thought he had the game locked up—and, for that matter, so did I. But I didn't give up, even though I was trailing by 140 points in a 125-point match. When it was my turn I ran 70-something points to bring me within about 60 points of

"Maybe if I study it a little more. . . ."

Dick. I took a good look at the score and at the situation on the table and told myself, "One more turn and I can pull this game out." So, confronted with a tough shot, I played safe. On his turn he didn't score, which gave me my big chance. I kept pocketing balls until I ran out. My sensational comeback put him into a state of shock—and it did me, too. The moral of the story is that, no matter how bad it looks, no matter how lopsided the score, keep giving the game your best shot.

Steve finally gives it a go . . .

When You're Far Ahead

Don't Let Down. When you're in the fortunate position of having a big lead you should never become careless and overconfident.

That's a problem I often run into. When I know I'm in control I tend to let up. Recently I was playing a fellow in a 100-point Straight Pool game, and I gave him a handicap so that he had to make only 55 points. Knowing I could win anytime, I held back and didn't concentrate as hard as I

. . . and even he . . .

should have. As a result, I missed a stupid little shot and he got back on the table and ended up winning by 15 points.

He beat me in the second game, too, though he really shouldn't have. Finally, in the third game, I played hard all the way and won easily.

Keep in mind that at one time or another, with a few breaks and a good handicap, just about any player can beat another. The game you ease up in is the one in which the guy you should easily beat is going to beat you. So, never let down.

. . . seems astonished at the results.

TIME TO PLAY

Sometimes crowds make people nervous, so I don't show up until I'm almost ready to play. If I have a game scheduled for eight o'clock, I see no purpose in getting there at seven.

I think most of the top players would agree. They get on the table and practice for 10-20 minutes and then want to get in there and play right away.

Incidentally, that prematch practice really has little to do with playing your game. You could miss everything on the table in practice and then get out there to play your game and *make* everything on the table. Or vice versa. It's like show business; often a bad dress rehearsal is followed by an excellent performance. The reason for the prematch practice is to loosen up your arm and fingers—and your nerves. I wouldn't recommend going in cold.

5

THE BIG TEST

In all the years I've spent at the pool table, I've noticed that certain game situations keep cropping up that challenge the skills and "smarts" of players of all levels. And I've seen players make the same mistakes over and over again.

As far as I'm concerned, the best test of whether or not a player is progressing to a more advanced level is how well he or she meets the challenges of these game situations and how he or she does in overcoming these mistakes.

On the following pages are illustrated descriptions of several of these problems and situations and tips on how I'd go about meeting them. Study them carefully, then duplicate them on the table and work on perfecting the solutions. Once you have these under control, you'll know you're well on your way to a higher level of play.

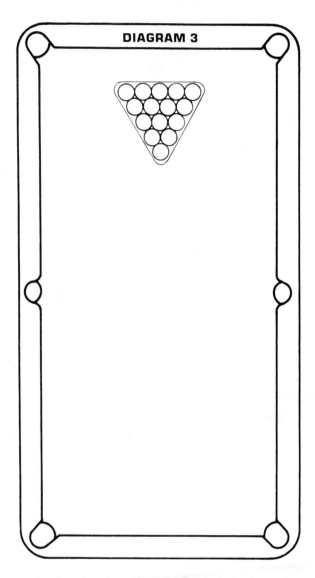

On the opening break, unless the rear five balls in the rack are absolutely frozen (touching without any space between them), you're going to open them up on the break and leave your opponent with a shot. In addition, if they're not touching, you might not manage to get two of them to the rail, which means you'll be penalized. If they're not touching, have the official or your opponent rerack them. All 15 balls should be frozen, but it's **imperative** that the back five be frozen.

STRAIGHT POOL

THE BREAK

In every game the break is very important. This is especially true in Straight Pool because, if you don't execute the opening break correctly, you may never get a chance to shoot again. I've often run out after my opponent broke, because he didn't break well. So try to break the very best you can.

As you stroke the cue on the opening break in Straight Pool, use as much right-hand English as you can and make the cue ball hit a quarter of the end ball in the last row of the rack. That ball is to the right as you face the rack. If you do it correctly, the cue ball will go down to the bottom rail, spin, come over to the short rail and back to the head rail. Corner balls will carom and return to the stack. That's the right way to break (see Diagram 6).

A common mistake players make is to position the cue ball improperly for the break. They place it either too close to the head spot or too close to the side rail (see Diagrams 4 and 5). Sometimes they fail to put sufficient English on the ball, or they hit the end ball too full or too thin, depending on where they've placed the cue ball. When the object ball is hit too full, the cue ball may end up scratching in the right corner pocket or too close to the rack of balls. Hit it too thin, and the cue ball will carom off the side rail and possibly scratch in another hole.

Many players neglect to check that the rear five balls in the rack are touching one another before the opening break. If they're not, you're headed for danger. You are probably going to open them up and leave your opponent with an easy shot, and you may not manage to get two of the object balls to the rail, in which case you'll be penalized. So have the referee or your opponent rerack the balls until those rear five are absolutely frozen (see Diagram 3). All 15 balls should really be frozen for the break, but the important ones are those last five.

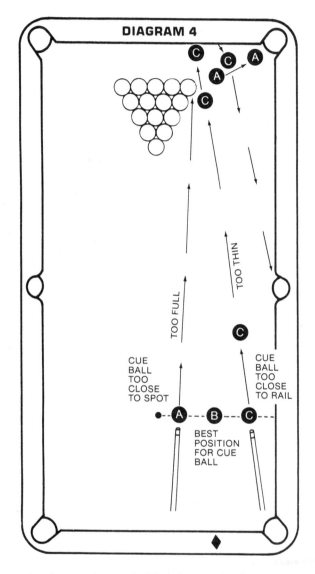

DIAGRAM 4

Players tend to line up the cue ball for the opening break either too close to the head spot (A), or too close to the side rail (C). When the cue ball is too close to the head spot, you're likely to hit the rear right corner object ball too full. The cue ball may then end up scratching in the right corner pocket. If you start out too close to the rail, you might·hit the end ball too thin. The cue ball is going to go off the side rail and go very long and wind up anywhere, possibly scratched in another hole.

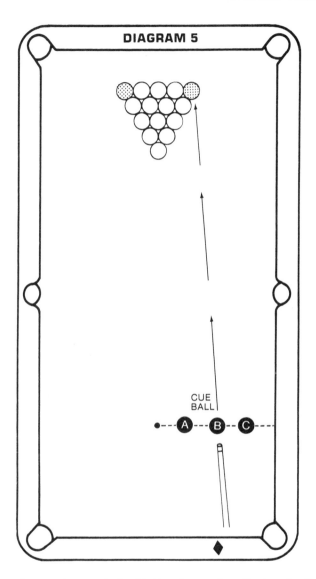

DIAGRAM 5

CUE
BALL

It's best to line up the cue ball with the diamond on the head rail and, using a lot of right-hand English, contact one-quarter of the ball in the rear right-hand corner.

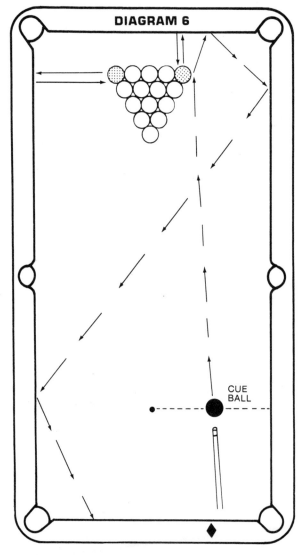

DIAGRAM 6

CUE
BALL

When you break correctly, the cue ball will contact one-quarter of the
ball in the rear right corner, causing that object ball to carom off the
foot rail and return to the stack. The ball at the opposite end of the last
row will carom off the left side rail and return to the stack. The cue ball,
meanwhile, will spin off the foot rail, into the right side rail, across to the
left side rail near the head of the table, and finally come to rest at the
head rail. This leaves your opponent with no shot—the ideal break.

STRATEGY

Assuming your opponent has broken and you're left with a display that looks like this (see Diagram 7), what should your course of action be?

Too many players think of position or other elements of the game rather than making the shot. Position play is all well and good, but remember, if you don't make that first shot, your turn is over.

Which ball do you aim for? The easier one, the ball (A) closer to the pocket. That's the one I'd recommend, even if it means the cue ball has to travel a longer distance than it would if you aimed for the object ball that wasn't quite as close to the pocket (ball B).

Before you take your shot, though, be sure to look over the rack for a possible combination shot. Often there's a combo that's dead in the hole that players overlook. In the example cited here (see Diagram 8) the combination is an easier shot than either single object ball.

When balls are all over the table, people often speculate that players are thinking five or even ten shots ahead. I think only a shot or two ahead, especially when all the balls are on the table.

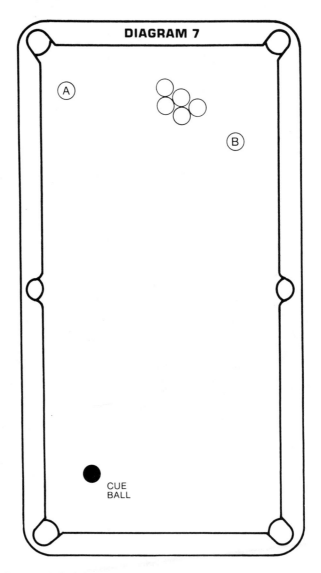

Given a choice between ball A and ball B, aim for A because it's closer to the hole—even though it requires a longer trip for the cue ball than ball B would.

In a situation like this—unless you're an advanced player willing to take a chance—shoot at the ball you're sure of making: the one nearest the pocket.

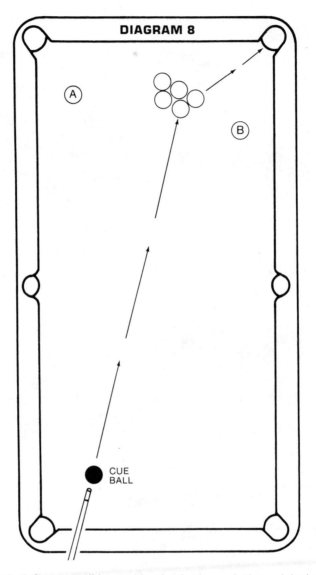

First look for a possible combination in the rack that might be the easiest shot of all.

TROUBLE SPOTS

In any event, you have to learn to spot trouble balls and open them up with the cue ball while pocketing another object ball. In the example shown here (see Diagram 9), pocket the object ball in the left side pocket and open up the trouble balls on the left rail.

It doesn't matter where they might have been clustered—on the rail, in the middle of the table, anywhere. You have to go after them and open them up as soon as possible. If you wait too long to do the dirty job, you're going to find that other object balls are too far away to pocket while breaking open the trouble balls. Then you'll be leaving the opportunities to your opponent. So go after the trouble balls as early as possible.

WILD CHANCES AND WILD CUE BALLS

You should never take wild chances, even if you're a good offensive-type player. You *can* play safe. But a lot of people, when playing safe off the rack of balls (see Diagram 10), don't make certain that balls 1 and 2 are frozen. The 1-ball will come out of the stack and hit the rail, and the others will stay in the stack as is—only if there is no space between balls 1 and 2. If they're not frozen—if there is space between those two balls—you might hit the 3 or other balls out of the stack and leave your opponent a shot. If the 1 and 2 are frozen, however, there's no such problem.

The less distance your cue ball travels, the better off you're going to be and the fewer shots you'll miss.

A common mistake less experienced players make is to let their cue ball run wild. People usually miss when they play long shots, so, obviously, shots that require the cue ball to travel a long distance should be avoided whenever possible. In fact, you should try to keep your cue ball from traveling past the side pocket; in other words, try to keep it within one half of the table (see Diagram 11).

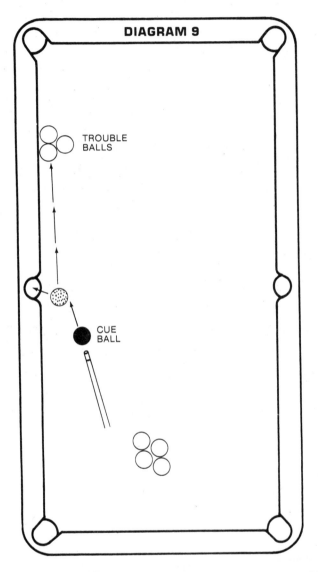

While pocketing the object ball in the side pocket, open up trouble balls.

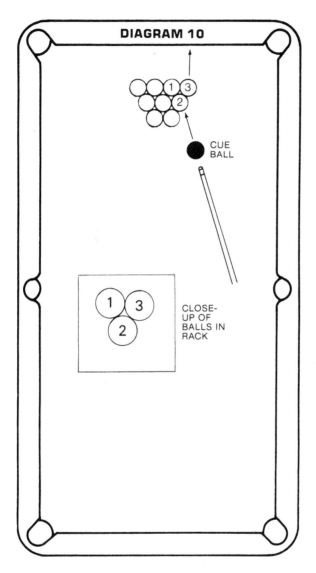

Don't take wild chances. You **can** play safe. But make sure the 1 and 2 balls are frozen, or you risk leaving your opponent with a shot.

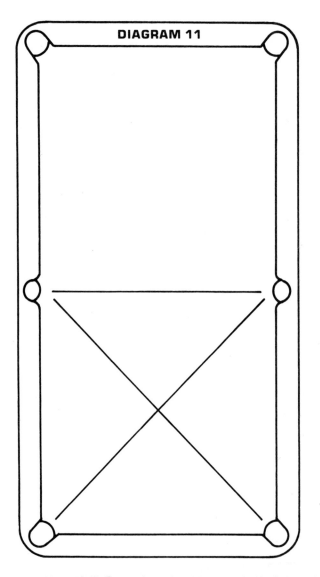

DIAGRAM 11

Don't have a wild cue ball. Try to keep it within one half of the table when a lot of balls are on the table and you are on the offense.

Besides missing shots, another problem often results from a wild cue ball: bad position. Better players don't hit many rails unless they absolutely have to. And when they do, they keep the number of rails to a minimum, through skillful use of English or hitting low or high.

Sure, there will be times when keeping the cue ball within one half of the table isn't possible—say a couple of object balls get to the top half of the table, while the rest are in the bottom. In that case, you'd clean out the top half as soon as possible and then carefully get it back to the bottom half— and keep it there.

DON'T TRY TO PINPOINT

Newer players make the mistake of trying to be too precise when they play position, and this leads to trouble.

Tom Watson can't tell you *exactly* where he's going to hit a golf ball; Jimmy Connors can't tell you the *exact* spot he's going to hit a tennis ball to. And we pool pros can't predict the *precise* location where our balls are going to land.

We can hit to within an inch or two of our target, within a general area. But not being machines or robots, we can't pinpoint the landing spot; so we allow ourselves a little leeway. To tell you the truth, in championship play we sometimes try to be exacting. But when you try to be *too* precise you end up overhitting or underhitting the ball or messing up your shot in some other way.

So don't put a strain on your brain; it's hard enough to make a shot without going crazy trying to play exact position. You're better off trying to get the cue ball to land in a general area rather than on a dime (see Diagram 12).

When I was growing up, I concentrated first on my shot making. When I could regularly make just about anything on the table, I started developing position play. I suggest you follow the same sequence.

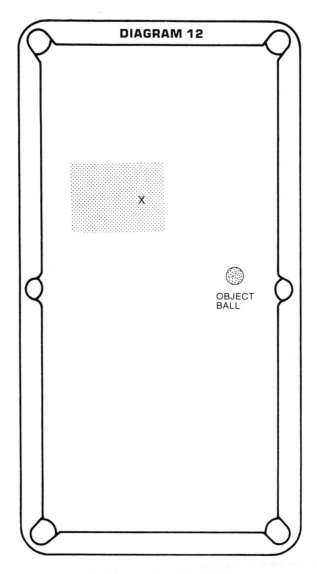

DIAGRAM 12

X

OBJECT
BALL

On position play, don't try to be too exact, or you'll mess up your shot. If the cue ball ends up anywhere in the shaded area, you'll have a good shot at the object ball in the side pocket. It doesn't have to land at the precise point X. Nobody is perfect.

BANK SHOTS

Take it from a professional show-off, the worst way to show off on a pool table is to try to shoot bank shots, especially when they're not necessary.

It's human nature to put on the dog a little—and pool players are maybe a little more human than others. So they try bank shots. And they miss bank shots. Avoid them at all costs.

Caroming a ball is much tougher than shooting a ball straight in, for the obvious reason that you have built-in interference—the rail. To hit off the rail successfully, you must make sure that the angle and everything else are perfect; there's really no margin for error. Consequently, a longer, seemingly tougher shot is often easier than a bank shot (see Diagram 13). I would rather take a straight-in shot at object ball 2, which is farther away, than take a bank shot with object ball 1.

Incidentally, for caroms or straight-in shots, few people realize that a corner pocket offers you a much wider target than a side pocket. With a corner pocket you can hit the ball into the railing edge or outside the railing edge, and the ball will still go in. With a side pocket the area open to you is considerably smaller. Consequently, a carom shot to a corner pocket has a better chance of succeeding than a carom shot to the side. You're still better off taking a straight-in shot.

If you're determined to try a carom shot, and you're faced with two possibilities (see Diagram 14), take the shorter bank of the two. Resist trying long-table banks, as impressive as they may seem. The ball has too far to travel.

BREAK BALL

Another name for Straight Pool, as you know, is 14.1, so-named because in the course of play, when there is one object ball remaining on the table, the other 14 balls are racked up.

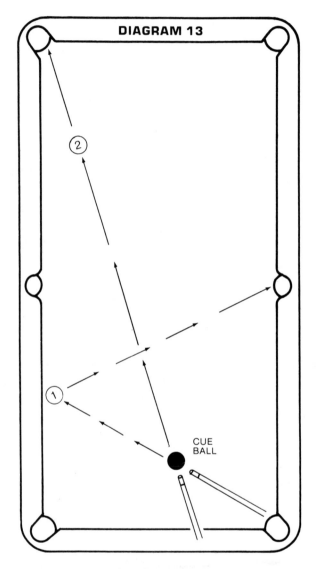

DIAGRAM 13

Resist showing off with bank shots. I'd rather try the longer straight-in shot, which may look tougher but has a better chance of success.

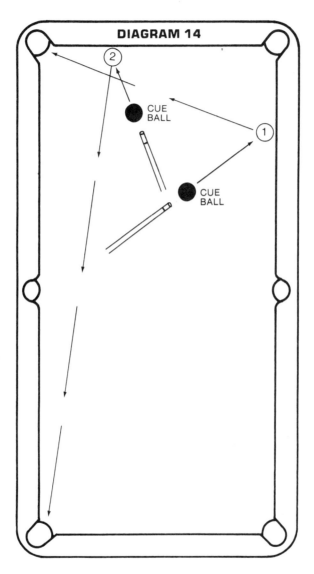

DIAGRAM 14

If you must try a bank shot, take the short-table one to a corner. Long-table banks should be avoided.

This is a pivotal point in the game, so you want to position yourself in such a way that you can pocket that last ball—the *break ball*—and break open the stack with the same shot and continue from there. Your chances of running up a high score or running out—winning the game—depend on whether you can keep going through the transition from when one or two balls are left on the table to when the other balls are reracked and all 15 are in play.

Which ball is going to be your break ball, the one you save for last before the reracking, is up to you. Usually your choice is a fairly obvious one. Keeping in mind that you want the cue ball to have to travel as short a distance as possible, you'll pick as the break ball one that is relatively close to the place where the other 14 will be racked.

The trick is to select your break ball (and, for that matter, the *key ball,* the one you'll sink immediately before the break ball) as early as possible—perhaps as soon as the opening break takes place (see Diagram 15). It's subject to change, of course. But the sooner you select it, the sooner—and better—you can work your strategy.

Think break ball, key ball, trouble balls, and get rid of the latter as soon as you can. Clear out one half of the table; get rid of your trouble balls that are along the rail or frozen together. Try to avoid sinking the break ball prematurely. But have an alternate break ball in mind. If you have to shoot them both, while there are other balls left on the table, then do so. You can always play safe, if need be.

If possible, though, leave the ball you've selected for last. Then sink it and break open the stack. (There's no rule, of course, that when the 14 balls are racked up, the break ball has to be pocketed first. But usually it's the most sensible approach.) And once the balls are broken, try to spot another break ball for the next round. This may seem to contradict what I said earlier about pros not thinking far ahead, but the break ball is an exception, an important one.

Once you become capable of picking a break ball, making the key shot, and getting into ideal position for the break shot, you're on your way to being a good player.

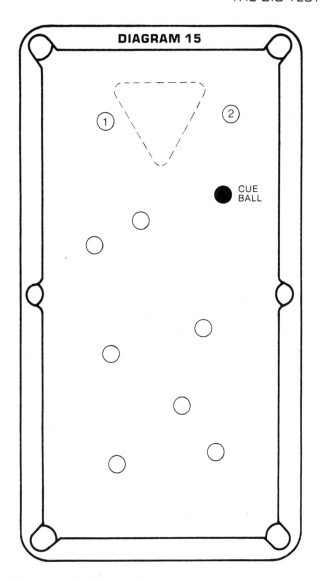

Think break ball (1 and alternate 2) as soon as possible.

An ideal break shot in 14.1.

A break shot in 14.1 that shouldn't be attempted. Play safe instead of trying to pocket a ball.

CONTROLLING THE CUE BALL

Often, a player will pocket the break ball, only to have the cue ball either stop dead in the stack or come way back to the other end of the table.

To prevent the cue ball from dying in the stack, put some English on it. And to make it do the job of opening up the stack and being in position to pocket additional balls, either draw it by hitting it low or follow it by hitting it high.

Some professional players draw the cue ball, while others follow it. I follow these guidelines: when the cue is to the left of an imaginary straight line to the object ball I hit it high; when it's to the right of that line I hit it low.

By hitting it high, you're going to have the cue ball go through the rack of balls and open them up (see Diagram 16). Unless you're very unlucky and go through all the balls and scratch, you really can't hit the cue *too* high.

If you hit the cue ball too low, however, you run the risk of having it come all the way back to the head of the table instead of breaking open the rack (see Diagram 17).

So beware of hitting it too low and make sure you apply some English. Remember, it's the deflection of the cue ball from the object ball that should be your main concern.

Now, let's summarize the points made thus far.

- On opening break, make sure rear balls are frozen.
- Look for dead combinations.
- Open trouble balls.
- Control the cue ball—don't let it run wild.
- In position play, don't be too exacting.
- Try straight-in shots rather than bank shots; if you *must* bank, aim for the corner pocket and take a short-table carom.
- Think about the break ball early.

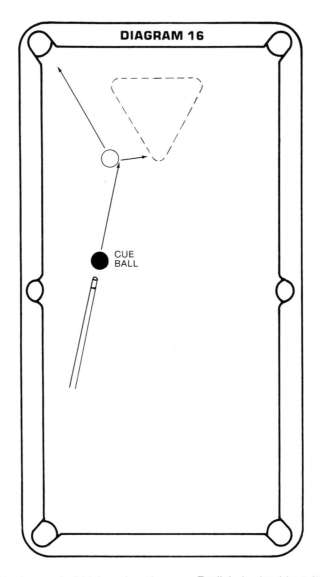

DIAGRAM 16

CUE
BALL

If you hit the cue ball high and apply some English, it should pocket the break ball, then open the stack and be in position to sink some of those balls. Remember, there is a little luck in everything you do.

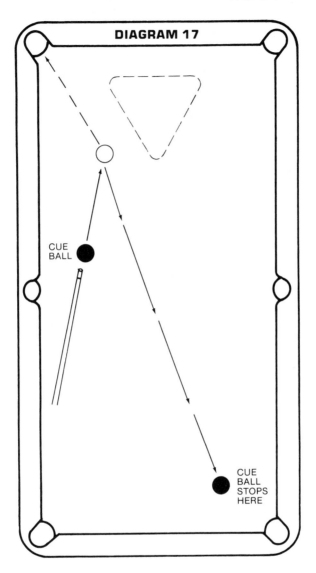

DIAGRAM 17

CUE
BALL

CUE
BALL
STOPS
HERE

If you hit the cue ball too low, it will sink the break ball but then will come back to the head of the table, which should not happen.

For the break in Nine-Ball, most of the better players today have a "floating cue ball," meaning they'll move it anywhere along the head string. Years ago, they'd position the cue ball right next to the head spot on the head string.

NINE-BALL

THE BREAK

Possibly the most important element in Nine-Ball is the opening break. Many times a good player will sink a ball on the break and then run out, with his opponent never getting a chance to shoot. If they'd agree to let me break, I'd give a lot of players a very good handicap in Nine-Ball.

Unlike the opening break in Straight Pool, where your main objective is not to leave your opponent with a good shot, in the Nine-Ball opening break you very definitely are trying to sink a ball. Sink a ball and have a shot at the next one.

Your best chance to accomplish this depends on whether *all* the balls in the rack are frozen (see Diagram 18).

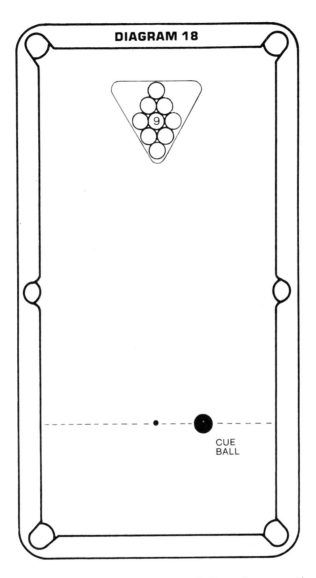

Make sure all nine balls in the rack in Nine-Ball are frozen on the break. Otherwise, the 9-ball won't move very far.

Remember, in Straight Pool it was imperative that the five balls at the rear of the rack be frozen. Well, in Nine-Ball, all nine have to be. That's your whole key. If you pocket a ball on the break and leave yourself with a shot, you're going to win; if you pocket a ball and don't leave yourself with a shot, you're going to lose. You'll probably lose, too, if you fail to make a ball on the break and leave your opponent with a shot. If you don't pocket a ball, but leave your opponent with nothing good to shoot at, you still have a good chance of winning.

If the balls in the rack are not frozen, they're likely not to travel as far when your cue ball contacts them. And if they're loose—as opposed to frozen—the 9-ball, being in the middle, is not going to move, and moving the 9-ball is what you really want to do. After all, it's the name of the game. So make sure all the balls in the rack are solid-frozen.

If you're lucky enough to win the chance to break, there are several points to keep in mind. Years ago players would position the cue ball right next to the head spot on the head string and hit the 1-ball in the rack straight on, contacting the cue ball just one tip above center. A few players still prefer to open that way, but most of the better players today have what they call a "floating cue ball" on break, which means they'll move it anywhere along the head string (see Diagram 19). But, from whatever point along the head string you hit the cue ball, you want to hit it a tip above center and have it strike the 1-ball flush (see Diagram 20). That way, the cue ball will carom away from the 1-ball a little bit and come to a dead stop, which is what you want it to do.

The major mistake people make on the break is having a wild cue ball, letting it fly off the table or scratch in a pocket. If either happens and you're playing a decent player, you're not going to be able to win. The key to avoiding these pitfalls is to control the cue ball. If necessary, sacrifice speed—but get control of that cue ball.

Wild cue balls occasionally plague even the best competitors. The last time I played Allen Hopkins, with the score

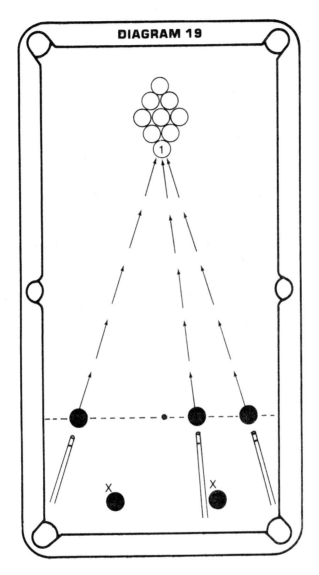

DIAGRAM 19

In the opening break in Nine-Ball, position the cue ball along the head string and stroke it a cue tip above center so that it strikes the 1-ball flush. Don't position the cue ball back near the head of the table, because then you'll lose velocity on impact.

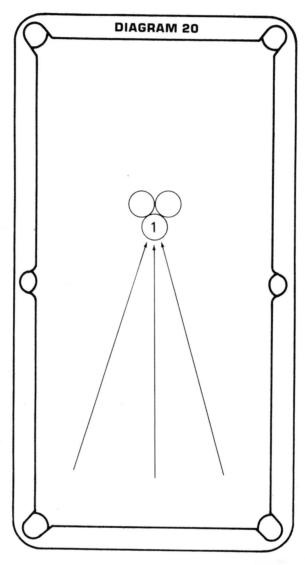

Close-up of where the cue ball should contact the 1-ball in the rack, depending on where on the head string the cue ball originated.

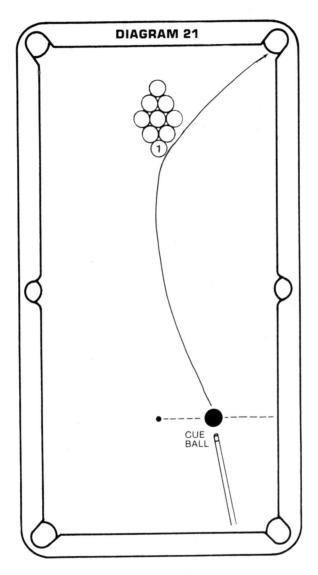

In Nine-Ball, if you don't hit the cue ball one tip above center and you don't control the cue ball, it will run wild and possibly scratch in the right or left corner pocket at the foot of the table.

10-10, he broke, and his cue ball jumped the table. He left me with a 1 and 9 combination. It was a tough shot, but I made it. His wild cue cost him the game.

I won that tournament in Houston, partly because I experimented with positioning the cue ball on the break. Early in the tournament I was breaking from the right side of the head string and not making anything. So I moved over to the left side and started making everything. The moral: if you're having trouble making balls with the cue ball positioned in one location on the break, move it somewhere else.

The one place you shouldn't move it, though, is back near the head rail (see Diagram 19). That's one of the worst things you can do, because then you lose power, and when you lose power you're sacrificing the strongest part of your break. Whenever you hit something, the velocity is greatest right at impact. The closer you get to the rack, the better—and the closest you can legally get on the break is to have your cue ball stationed along the head string.

So get your cue ball as close to the rack as possible and hit it with authority, but without having it go wild. In other words, sacrifice a little speed and power for control, which is the most important thing; if you don't have control, you're dead.

STRATEGY

The rules of Nine-Ball will often determine your strategy. As you know, you have to pocket the balls in rotation or play a combination with the 9-ball or another ball by means of a carom shot. You have to choose correctly between the straight-in shot and the combination.

Often, inexperienced players like to make the 9-ball very early, to show off their skill, but that could be the wrong thing to attempt. If you have the ability to run the nine balls in succession, why risk the combination shot? It's as dangerous in Nine-Ball as it is in Straight Pool. Unless the

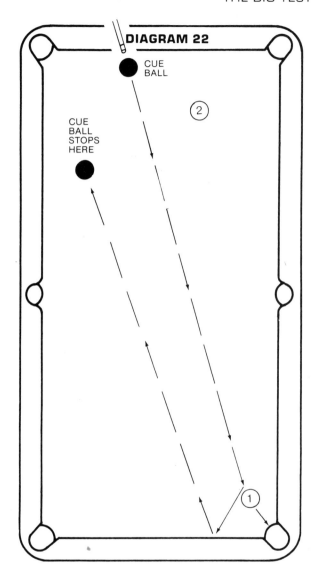

Pocket ball 1 and get into position for ball 2.

combination is dead in the hole, or there's no other shot possible, don't shoot the combination.

I grant you, the combination is often tempting, especially because, if it consists of the 1-ball and 9-ball, for example, either one can go in first and you'll still win. In fact, the 1-ball doesn't even have to go in the pocket, as long as the ball you hit first in the combination is the one that's due in rotation. (If the 1-ball has already been pocketed, that would be the 2-ball, and so on.) But as tempting as it is, resist the temptation.

TROUBLE SPOTS

Risking dangerous temptations is only one of the mistakes to avoid that are common to Nine-Ball *and* Straight Pool. Trouble balls are another. But there are some differences. In both games there will be times when you want to leave trouble balls alone because you can't make them. But when they are playable you have to remember in Nine-Ball that you must play position on the next-numbered ball rather than on any ball.

As noted, sometimes it's wiser to play safe than to try to pocket a trouble ball (see Diagram 26). In the example shown here, you're better off to play safe. Strike the cue ball so it contacts the lone object ball and drives it off the foot rail and side rail, so it comes to rest near the head of the table toward the right corner pocket. The cue ball, meanwhile, will carom off the object ball, then off the foot rail, and come to rest immediately behind the cluster of balls. This leaves your opponent without a good shot. He can't hit the object ball at the head of the table, because the cue is behind the cluster. But, under the rules by which we play today, he has to *try* to hit the object ball, because it's the next number in rotation. If he fails to hit it, you have cue ball in hand, meaning—as you know—that you can place it *anywhere* on the table. So, obviously, in this instance, playing safe was a much better choice for you than trying to pocket a ball.

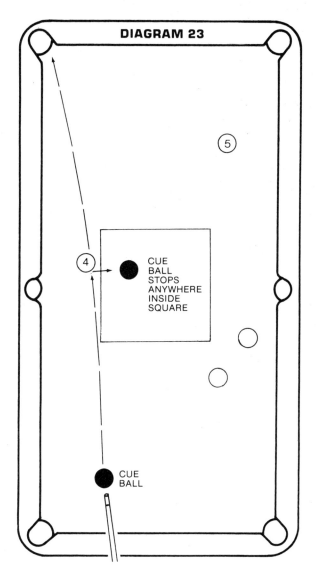

DIAGRAM 23

4

5

CUE
BALL
STOPS
ANYWHERE
INSIDE
SQUARE

CUE
BALL

In this Nine-Ball game, by trying too hard to get into position for the 5-ball, you risk missing the straight-in shot on the 4-ball. So be sure you make the 4. And, rather than try to pinpoint your exact position, try to have the cue ball land in a general area from which you can either make the 5 or play safe.

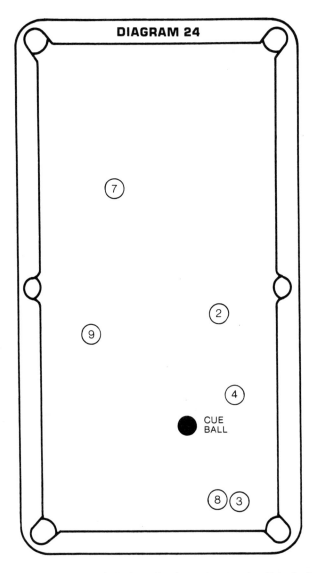

The problem in this Nine-Ball situation is to get on the 3-ball after sinking the 2-ball. I would try to pocket the 2 in the side by using high left-hand English and try to break open the 3 and the 8, or I would shoot the 2 in the corner and use low right-hand English.

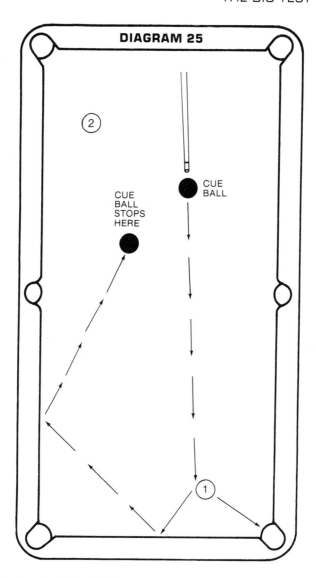

In this situation in a Nine-Ball contest, my objective is not only to sink the 1-ball, but to get into position to sink the 2-ball. Therefore, I'll drive the cue ball against the head rail so that it will brush the 1-ball into the pocket and when it caroms off end in the half of the table where the 2-ball is located.

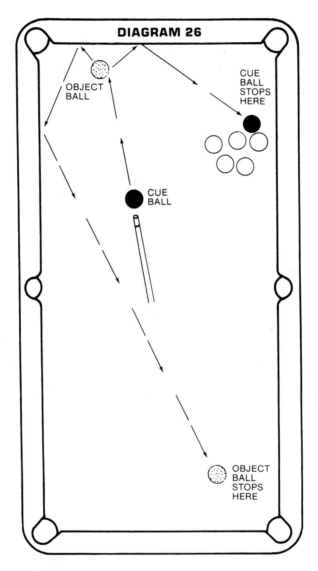

DIAGRAM 26

OBJECT
BALL

CUE
BALL
STOPS
HERE

CUE
BALL

OBJECT
BALL
STOPS
HERE

Sometimes it's better to play safe rather than try to make a difficult shot. By driving the lone object ball off two rails and having the cue ball land behind the cluster of balls, you leave your opponent with an impossible shot.

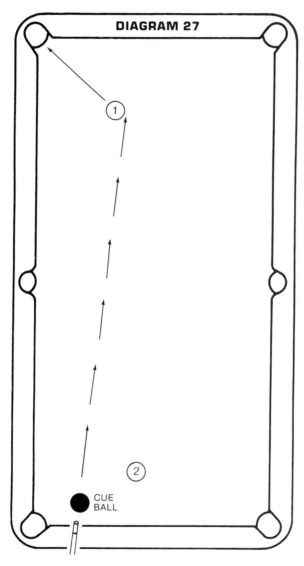

With the 1-ball so far from the cue ball, it's a tough shot. Chances of pocketing the ball and getting position are slim, but it **can** be done. You have the option of playing safe, but if you think you can make the shot, go for it. Remember, even if you play safe, your opponent can leave you safe on the next shot.

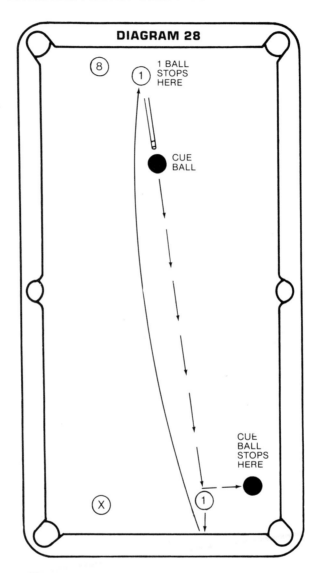

DIAGRAM 28

In a setup like this, where you have only a slim possibility of making a shot, I would weigh the chances of missing against playing safe. My choice would be to play safe by hitting the cue ball into the 1-ball, driving the 1-ball against the rail and having it end almost at the foot rail, near the 8-ball. The cue ball, meanwhile, caroms off the 1-ball and ends near the right side rail toward the foot of the table. This is what's called a **speed shot,** one that you really have to control.

THINKING AHEAD

When you play Nine-Ball you must have in mind what your next shot is going to be. In fact, you ought to have a mental picture of the whole pattern—not only the 1, 2, 3, 4, 5, 6, 7, and 8, but the 9-ball as well, because if you don't sink the 9, sinking all the others doesn't mean anything. Don't be fancy and try to make every tough shot on the table. If you don't have a shot, or the only one available is really tough, play safe. If your opponent is a smart player, you'll have plenty of *kicks* (chances) at the ball.

PRACTICE: THREE-CUSHION BILLIARDS

A good game to practice in preparation for playing Nine-Ball is Three-Cushion Billiards. It's played with two white balls and a red ball on a table that has no pockets. Because it's essentially a carom game, it's ideal training for Nine-Ball, which involves a lot of caroms, since players are always trying to snooker you (leave you unable to shoot in a straight line at an object ball because of the way other balls are located on the table).

LOTSA LUCK

There's a lot of luck involved in Nine-Ball. I've been in a position where I was snookered but managed to kick the cue ball off two side rails to hit a ball and leave my opponent snookered. You really never know what's going to happen.

In general, though, the fewer rails you hit, the less likely you are to scratch. If you can limit your play to half of the table, your scratch potential is reduced to four pockets, so you've eliminated a third of the places you might scratch. And the sure-to-be-fatal kind of shot to avoid is blasting the cue ball so hard that it jumps off the table. If it does, you're dead.

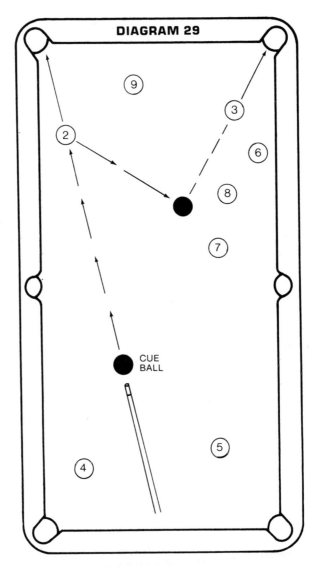

The challenge in this setup in Nine-Ball is to get into position to pocket the 2-ball, then the 3-ball, and then the 4-ball. In sinking the 2-ball, draw the cue ball back about two feet, so you can have the 3-ball straight in.

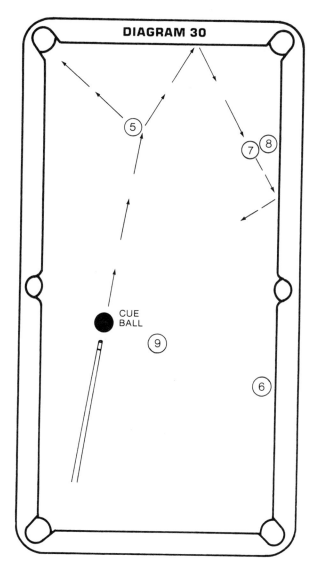

The 7-ball and 8-ball spell trouble, and somehow I'm going to break them up. Unless I do, I can't win. While you are pocketing the 5, carom off the 7, as shown here.

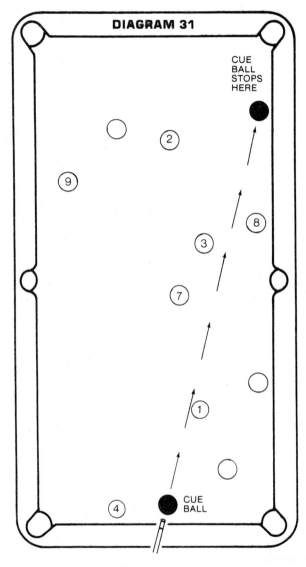

DIAGRAM 31

Deciding to play safe in this Nine-Ball situation, have the cue ball just brush the 1-ball and settle against the right-hand rail at the far end of the table.

DON'T PLAY **TOO** SAFE

With all my emphasis on playing safe, I have to point out an inherent danger. There are occasions when players concentrate so much on playing safe that they overlook excellent opportunities for making a shot. I've seen players fail to shoot at, say, the 6-ball, which was right in the corner near the pocket, and play safe. Had they pocketed the 6-ball, they might have gone on to run out. Instead, they played safe and ended up losing.

It happened between Allen Hopkins and me, in that game I mentioned earlier. There he was, one of the greatest Nine-Ball players in the world, and he let a shot go, because he felt he couldn't make the ball and run out. When he played safe I hit the ball and snookered him.

The message here is that, in Nine-Ball, a bird in the hand is worth two in the bush. Before playing safe, make certain you're not overlooking a shot that could lead you to victory.

In my opinion, Nine-Ball is essentially an offensive game, one that favors a player like Mike Sigel, who has an extremely powerful offense and can make shots from almost anywhere. A great defensive Straight Pool player like Irving Crane has a good offense when he's close to the balls, but his long-shot ability is not as good as Mike's, and, consequently, Mike will run more racks than Irving will.

Unlike Straight Pool, Nine-Ball exacts no penalties for playing safe. You can play safe three times in a row and snooker your opponent, and if he doesn't hit the next ball in rotation, you'll win the game without making the 9-ball.

WINNING BIG

Nine-Ball is a very fast game and very entertaining for spectators. Because it goes so quickly, it's a good, popular betting game.

Because luck is such a big element in Nine-Ball, a lesser player has a better chance of winning an occasional game from a better player in Nine-Ball than in Straight Pool or

Eight-Ball. But if you're playing an opponent who's better than you, don't let the prospect of scoring an upset carry you away; too many lesser players bet too much on themselves in Nine-Ball. While you might win a game here and there, over a series the better player is going to win most of the contests.

Whether you're better or worse than your opponent, or about even with him or her, try very hard to win the first two or three games of, say, a *Race to 10* (as a *whoever-wins-10-first* series is called). Jumping out to the early lead builds your confidence, shakes your opponent's, and makes it very tough for him to recover. A 3-0 lead in a 10-game Nine-Ball tournament is much more significant than a 30-0 lead is in Straight Pool.

OK, you say, you'll try to win those first two or three Nine-Ball contests, but you try to win *every* game you play. All I can tell you is *concentrate* from the word *go*. If you let yourself get into the match gradually, you may suddenly realize you're behind 5-0 and never recover.

MIND GAMES

Playing against a great safe player like Allen Hopkins can play tricks on your mind. He's so good at snookering you that you may never get a chance to shoot at a ball straight into the hole. That alone affects your thinking and mental balance. Another effect it has is that when you do get a decent shot at a ball you worry that this is the only shot you're going to get, so you better make it good—or else. Needless to say, that doesn't help your chances.

What you have to do is take advantage of what you've got—your shot—because what really controls the situation is the balls. If your opponent leaves you safe, you can't do anything about it. But if he misses and leaves you with a straight-in shot, you're on your way. Not to put undue pressure on you, you better make that shot or risk not getting another one for 10 games.

Sometimes it's better to play safe and hope to get cue ball in hand, rather than try to run out and have to worry about getting into position for the next ball. Here, the 1-ball is a fairly tough shot so, rather than try to pocket it and get position on the 3-ball, he'll hit the 1-ball and try to freeze the cue ball behind the 6-ball.

Voila, his opponent is snookered behind the 6-ball.

A rule that has been introduced in recent years for Nine-Ball tournaments (as well as Eight-Ball and Seven-Ball) makes the game very interesting but also very nerve-wracking. Previously, if (after the break) you scratched or didn't hit the ball you were aiming at, your opponent would get the cue ball behind the head string. Under the new rule, however, he gets the ball in hand anywhere on the table. That's obviously a tremendous advantage. If a scratch occurs on the break, he still only gets to put the cue ball in play behind the head string.

TOURNAMENT NINE-BALL

Tournament play in Nine-Ball takes the form of Hit-the-Ball, which means you have to hit the next ball in rotation or you are severely penalized. Your opponent gets the cue ball in hand anywhere on the table. This differs from the big bettors' favorite, which is known as One-Shot Shootout. In this game you're allowed to stroke the cue ball and not hit an object ball, without being penalized. In this form of Nine-Ball your opponent then can try the tough shot you've left him or her with, or declare that he or she wants you to try it. If your opponent lets you take it, and you miss, he or she then gets the cue ball in hand anywhere on the table, which usually spells the end.

HUSTLER'S PET

Nine-Ball is a favorite game of hustlers. Each contest is over so quickly that they can easily pretend to be inferior players—until the betting gets up to the big-bucks level. Especially in a four-handed game of Nine-Ball, hustlers will play like rank amateurs for several games while their opponents just about trip over themselves trying to up the ante and bleed this apparent "sucker." But when the ante gets high enough to make it worth their while, hustlers show their true playing ability and demonstrate who the real suckers are.

If you're a spectator looking for gambling action at a

Nine-Ball match, and you have suspicions that one of the contestants is a hustler, you'd be wise to hold off on your betting until the time is ripe for the hustler to reveal himself. Then place your bet accordingly. Otherwise, just bet on the player who seems to have the confidence and the skill to back up that confidence.

Better yet, get into the game yourself.

ONE-POCKET

One-Pocket, the game in which you and your opponent each pick a single pocket as your own before the game begins, is a totally defensive game. A player who has great defense and good offense is very, very dangerous in this game, because all it requires is for you to sink eight balls in the pocket you've selected.

The best way to accomplish your objective in One-Pocket is to force your opponent to make a mistake, and the way to do that is to put him in some *hellaceous* (dreadful) position. Do that, and you'll have the upper hand at all times.

Most likely, you'll each pick one of the pockets at the foot of the table.

THE ALL-IMPORTANT BREAK

The break is the most important element in the game, because if you don't execute it properly, you're going to lose. It brings with it a very big advantage because it usually enables the shooter to put four or five balls near his designated pocket, and leaves his opponent in a very precarious position.

Before you shoot the opening break, make sure that the balls in the rack are lined up straight, not tilted to one side. If any of the five balls along the outside edge of the triangle, on the side from which you're shooting, is out of line, the cue ball is likely to kick into a pocket.

Be sure that the five balls along that outer edge are frozen as close as possible (see Diagram 32), so you don't mistak-

Uh-oh. Steve's opponent has made an excellent break in One-Pocket and put him in a hellish position. What should he do in this dreadful predicament?

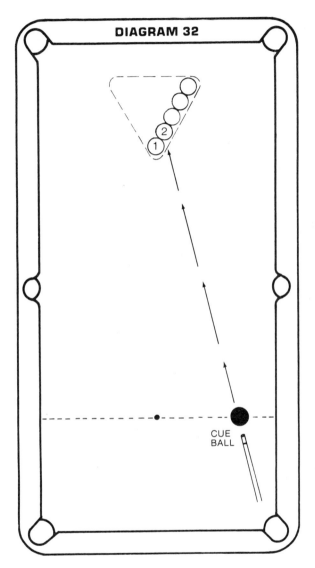

On the opening break in One-Pocket, make sure the five balls along the edge of the rack (on the side from which you're shooting) are frozen and that the whole rack is straight, not tilted. Place the cue ball on the head string about four or five inches from the side of the rail diagonally opposite your pocket. Hit the cue ball with high left-hand English because the cue is on the right side of the rack.

enly sink balls in your opponent's pocket (which would count for your opponent) or scratch.

Once the balls are racked to your satisfaction, place the cue ball along the head string, about four or five inches from the side rail. Which side you place the cue ball at will be determined by which pocket you've chosen. If it's the one at the left-hand corner of the foot rail, you'll place your cue ball at the right side of the head spot. You do this because you have the best chance of pocketing balls in the pocket diagonally across from where the cue ball originates.

Assuming your pocket is in the left corner so you've placed the cue ball on the head string four or five inches from the right rail, you would stroke it with high left-hand English, aiming for the point between the first and second ball along the right side of the triangle. Like a bowler trying for a strike, you want to hit that spot rather than the first ball (or pin) head on.

If your pocket is at the right corner, you place the cue ball to the left and hit between the first and second balls on *that* side.

EXECUTION AND STRATEGY

Most times in One-Pocket a player knows what he has to do, but can't execute the stroke. For example, he knows the cue should be splitting the first two balls, but he strokes and either hits the first ball too full or misses it entirely and hits the second ball. If you're not executing properly, a whole bunch of players will beat you on your mistakes. But if you are able to execute properly with the cue ball, no one is going to beat you.

One-Ball is often compared to a game of chess in that you move, then your opponent countermoves, and then you try to nullify his or her move with one of your own. You have to get a ball either over by your pocket or into some position where your opponent can't get it going toward his or her pocket.

Generally, as long as you can keep making balls go toward your pocket, you'll be doing pretty well in the game.

When your opponent has balls near his or her pocket, you ordinarily have two options. If the shot is relatively easy, take it, because the "bird-in-the-hand" philosophy applies as much in One-Pocket as it does in Nine-Ball. But if the shot isn't easy, rather than take a chance on missing, get rid of those balls that are near your opponent's pocket.

As long as you keep your opponent on the defensive, you'll probably win the game.

In the instance in which you have a very difficult, if not impossible, shot (see Diagram 33) you might do better to knock the balls away from your opponent's pocket than try to sink a ball in your pocket. But you have to be careful that the cue ball ends in a position where your opponent won't be able to bank the ball near your pocket into his pocket. In the situation illustrated in the diagram you would hit the left side of ball 1 so that it caromed off the foot rail into ball 2, and they both end away from your opponent's pocket. The cue ball, meanwhile, stops frozen to the foot rail, a very safe position in that your opponent doesn't have a bank on your ball.

A common mistake beginning players make in One-Pocket—and in other games, for that matter—is that they think they have to drill a bank shot. If you hit a bank too hard, the object ball is likely to carom off the rail near the pocket you were aiming for and end up near the opposite pocket, your opponent's (see Diagrams 34 and 35).

In One-Pocket you have to make your shots count and exploit every opportunity. If there's a chance to make a ball, make it. If there's a chance to run six, don't stop at two. Players will sink a ball but fail to get into proper position for the next shot. It's happened to me, where I should be able to run eight, and I end up running four and losing.

The point is, to win at One-Pocket, you have to take full advantage of every chance you get. To do that, you have to play with gusto.

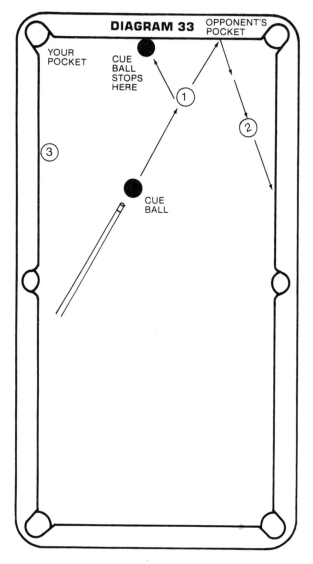

Sometimes you'll do better trying to knock balls away from your opponent's pocket than trying to pocket one in your own. But be sure the cue ball ends up in a place that won't allow your opponent a bank shot on your ball.

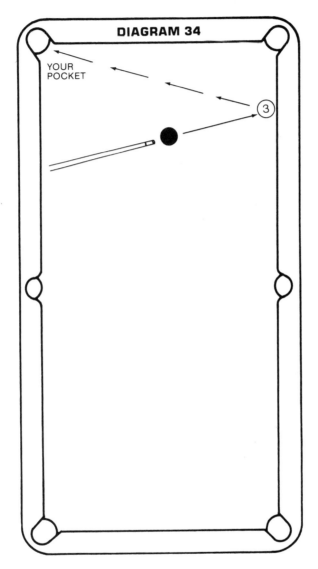

If you hit a bank shot with medium velocity, you should make the ball in
the intended pocket or make it stop by your pocket.

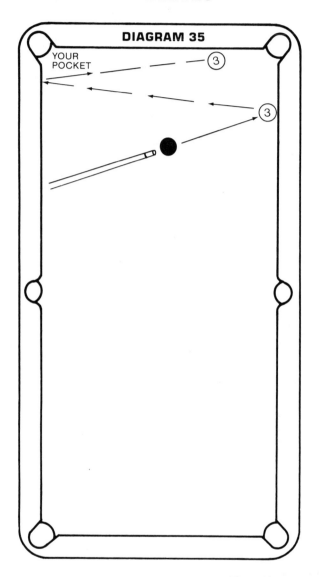

DIAGRAM 35

YOUR
POCKET

If you hit it too hard, the object ball is likely to carom off the rail near your pocket and end up near your opponent's pocket.

EIGHT-BALL

As any pool player who's been paying attention knows, the object of Eight-Ball is to pocket a specific 7 of the 15 object balls (either 1–7 or 9–15) and then the 8-ball before your opponent sinks his or her 7 and then the 8-ball. You don't have to call any shots except the one involving the 8-ball. Of course, if you sink the 8-ball on the opening break, you automatically win the game.

THE BREAK

The pros are using a new break in Eight-Ball, which they feel gives them a better chance of winning the game on the break. Instead of having the cue ball hit the top of the rack, they make it hit the second ball down and draw into the side rail (see Diagram 37). That way, they're moving all the balls. When you hit from the side your chance of making a

When the balls are racked for a game of Eight-Ball, the 8-ball should be in the middle of the third row, and the striped and solid object balls separated as much as possible.

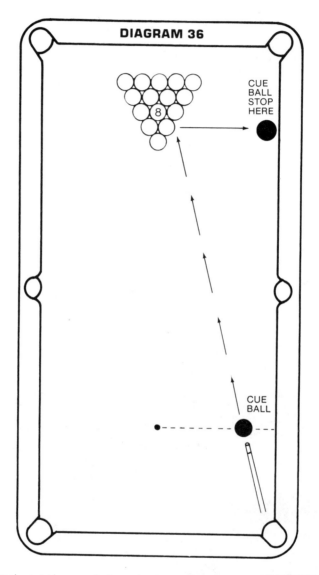

DIAGRAM 36

If you break, put the cue ball on the head string near the right side and break into the second ball on the right side of the rack, drawing the cue ball into the side rail.

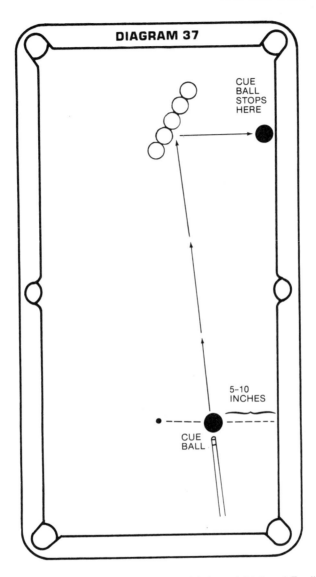

DIAGRAM 37

CUE
BALL
STOPS
HERE

5–10
INCHES

CUE
BALL

On the Eight-Ball break, hit the cue ball with low right-hand English and aim it directly at the second ball along the right side of the rack. The cue ball should end up at the side rail.

ball is a lot greater; in addition, when you hit from the side a lot of balls carom off the rail, come back into the stack, and move the 8-ball. You have a better chance of pocketing the 8-ball when you hit from the side than when you hit from the front. I once saw the 8-ball get pocketed on the break three times in a row, but that is as rare as a hustler's returning a sucker's money voluntarily. You can get rich giving big odds against its happening.

You should place the cue ball on the head string, about 10 inches from the right side rail, and stroke with low, left English, or from the left side and stroke with low, right English.

Because the choice of the group of balls isn't made until after the opening break, you should drive the cue ball as hard as you can on the break, to sink as many balls as possible. If you sink more balls in the 1–7 category than you do of the 9–15 group, then, of course, you'll select that group as yours. If you fail to sink any balls on the break, your opponent gets to choose which group is his.

If your opponent breaks and fails to sink any balls, it's your turn to pick, and your choice should be based on which of the balls are in a better position for you to pocket.

CAREFUL!

You can lose the game in a lot more ways than you can win it. For example, you lose if:

- (except on the break) you pocket the 8-ball before you've pocketed all seven of your other numbered balls;
- you're trying to make the 8-ball and it goes into a different pocket than the one you designated;
- you're shooting for the 8-ball, but on that shot the cue hits another ball before the 8-ball is pocketed;
- you scratch the cue ball in a pocket when shooting to make the 8-ball.

All these ways to lose can make you crazy. But if you keep

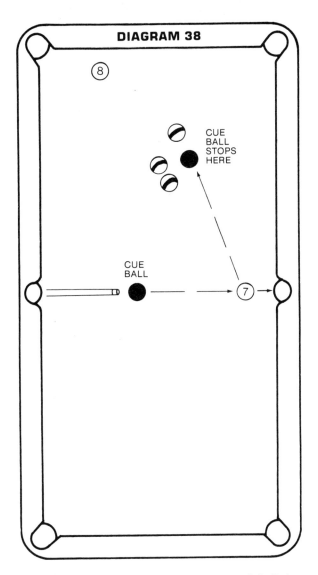

In Eight-Ball, make sure before you pocket your seventh ball that you'll be able to sink the 8-ball. In this case the player makes the seventh ball, but the cue ends up behind a cluster of the opponent's balls.

Steve takes time to plan in this Eight-Ball game. The last solid ball (his to sink) on the table is an easy shot. But he's better off not trying to sink it because he won't be able to get into position to pocket the 8-ball.

your cool and follow some time-tested advice, you can avoid ending up "behind the 8-ball."

STRATEGY

You may be rolling along, pocketing one ball after another in your designated group and have just one left. But make sure, before you pocket the seventh of your group of balls, that you'll be able to sink the 8-ball. If you sink the seventh ball but end up behind a cluster of your opponent's balls (see Diagram 38), you'll be in trouble. If you can't hit the 8-ball, you'll lose your turn, and, with all your seven balls off the table, your opponent will probably have an easy time finishing off his remaining balls and then the 8-ball.

I've often played games in which it's agreed that I get to break, and all my opponent's balls are off the table, and he's credited with them. It seems like a big advantage for my opponent, but actually the advantage is mine, because he has taken away any interference—his balls were the only thing that could have stopped me from going all the way.

Getting back to my point about not going after the seventh ball unless you have a good chance of making the 8-ball, I would even suggest not making your sixth ball if the 8-ball is tied up. You can't really play safe when you've got only one ball left, so, depending on your skill and self-confidence, you either deliberately avoid pocketing the seventh and perhaps the sixth ball, waiting for your opponent to break the balls open a little, or you sink the seventh and try to break open the 8-ball, even though you know you can't sink it. Often, the best thing to do is to hold back and see what your opponent does. He's liable to run five of his balls and then have to leave two frozen to the 8. Then he'll have nothing left, and you'll be able to finish the job.

6

POOLROOM CHARACTER TYPES
WHICH OF THEM IS YOU?

In the course of a night in your neighborhood poolroom you're bound to see every conceivable personality type, from conservative to spacy, from amiable to hostile, from icy to spasmodic. These types—or reasonable facsimiles thereof—show up anywhere there's a pool table, and they're so common that we've given them nicknames. In some instances, their pool-playing personalities are the very factor that does them in at the table, the element that keeps them from being better players, the difference between winning and losing.

As you read about these types, ask yourself very honestly whether one or more of them might be you. If your answer is yes, start figuring out how to keep that quirk under control so it doesn't beat you at the game.

Here are some of the common species found in billiard parlors. Recognize them?

SOREHEAD SAL/GRUMPY GUS

At the end of one match, instead of shaking hands as you're supposed to, two notorious soreheads exchanged nasty words. The argument escalated to the point that one of the players picked up his cue case, batted his opponent on the back of the head with it, and knocked him three rows back into the stands. That should never happen, but it did, and I think both of them regretted it (especially, I'm sure, the one who ended up in the stands).

This is an extreme example, I grant you, but it's typical of what we see too often: the chronic complainer who's always blaming everything and everyone but himself for his playing errors. He'll play bad position, or blow a hanger, or scratch, but he's convinced it wasn't his fault; it happened, he's sure, because of the crowd, the table, the lighting, his opponent, or the referee.

In a U.S. Open final I was shooting straight over the ball, and my cue stick came down and touched the top of it. The ball didn't even move. Only one person in the room thought it was a foul, but he happened to be the referee, so I was called for it. I couldn't believe the "foul" call—but that's show (or pocket billiards) business, and I had to accept it.

In another tournament I put my hand down on the tablecloth, and I was maneuvering my fingers around as I prepared to shoot. I never touched a ball, but finger movements caused the cloth to move and in turn made the cue ball move. Even though I hadn't touched the cue ball, the referee called me for a foul. It was really a bad call, and it cost me my turn and a point. (I also lost the tournament, but not that game.) Yet I had to accept it and not lose my cool. Not everybody has that much self-control.

Some Grumpy Guses will complain about their handicaps after a game is over. Let's say, for example, I spot you a certain number of points, based on our respective track records. There's always a certain amount of negotiation involved in establishing the point spread, but eventually there's agreement. Let's say, for purposes of this example, I spot you 40 points, but you play way below your usual level, and I beat you by 75. If you're like some of these Sorehead Sals, you'll moan and groan that I didn't spot you enough.

For the way you played this particular game, you're right—but based on past performance, you don't have a legitimate gripe.

Being the last angry man when you play pool can defeat you. It can keep you from analyzing your shortcomings objectively and working to overcome them. Sure, it's easier to be sore and to holler about how everything was against you. But that doesn't do anything to help your game.

BOOZER BILL

Just as you can't drink and drive, you can't drink and play winning pool. Boozing has ruined individual matches, major tournaments, and even whole careers. It's very sad to see.

You may believe that drinking will help relax you—and maybe it does for a short time—but it soon ruins your concentration, your table "smarts," and your aim, among other skills. If you're bombed, you'll bomb out.

I'm happy to say that a lot of players who were having a bottle problem have cleaned up their act and gone on to realize their full potential in pocket billiards. But others have not been so lucky, and they've shot their careers in a shot glass.

HUSTLIN' HUMPHREY

There are scores of pool players loose in the world who are just dying to get into your pockets—via the pockets on a pool table. If you're not sharper than they are, they'll succeed.

The basic problem in protecting yourself against Hustlin' Humphrey and fellows like him is that he may be very hard to identify. The hustler wears no scarlet letter H on his shirt to warn you to beware. In fact, the most successful hustlers don't bear the slightest resemblance to your preconception of a hustler—certainly not at first. In fact, a hustler will often seem to be the friendliest guy in the world.

Traditionally, hustlers let their opponents win at the beginning to encourage them to keep playing, at higher stakes. Eventually the hustlers make their kill. How do you protect yourself?

I go into the defenses against hustling in great detail in a special section of my book, *Steve Mizerak's Pocket Billiards Tips and Trick Shots,* published by Contemporary Books, Inc. Let me give you a quick synopsis here.

Your best protection is not betting. If you don't bet, you can't be hustled, and you can't lose. Of course, you can't win either, so you'll probably ignore the advice not to bet.

The next best defense is to play and bet only with players you know. Even if a stranger strikes you as a great human being, avoid playing pool with him for money. Expert hustlers have been known to invest days or weeks ingratiating themselves with the billiard-parlor denizens before suggesting "friendly" games, at small stakes, which they lose. Eventually, though, they'll start winning and clean you out.

If you find yourself in a game in which you suspect you're being hustled, stop playing as soon as you can—even before you win any money and certainly before you lose. It's hard to walk away while the tide is still running in your favor, but do it at all costs. If you must, invent a wife having a baby, a sick uncle, a Simon Legree boss, but get away from that hustler as soon as you can.

It's unlikely that hustlers will be carrying fancy, custom-made cues, but there are other giveaways: they will want to raise the stakes after you've won half a dozen games in a row, for example. Oversincerity is another clue. Earl Schriver, who made a lifetime living through pool hustling, was so sincere that when he'd say, "You look fine today;

let's fool around on the table for a couple of dollars," few could resist playing him. And very quickly he'd have the stakes well up from those "few" dollars. He was a superb player, but he was so effective in the way he touted his lack of ability that strangers believed him—and spotted him such great odds he couldn't help but win.

The townspeople would protest, "You're too good," and, good sport that he was, he'd agree to less of a handicap. He kept winning until finally he had to give *them* odds. He left one particular town with a few thousand dollars he hadn't arrived with—and this a town you wouldn't expect to get $15 out of.

Maybe you want to be the hustler yourself and beat the hustler at his own game. But you have to know when to lose and when to win, without tipping your hand. You have to have a good measure of self-confidence and the ability to support that confidence, without being *overconfident*. And, above all, to succeed at hustling—or even friendly wagering—you have to be at least as good at *making* the game as you are at *playing* it. Give away too much of a handicap and you'll erase whatever playing superiority you have over an opponent. For instance, even if you're 10 times the player your opponent is, if you give him a handicap in which he has to get only 10 points to win while you need 100, there's too great a chance that you'll miss before you get to 100 and he makes his 10.

With the right handicap almost any good player can beat another, which reinforces the contention that a good game *maker* can beat a good game *player*. So haggle as long as necessary to make a game you can win.

And, whatever you do, don't invest in a hustler. In other words, don't let yourself be conned into backing a hustler. At best, you're risking all the money, while he's risking only pride. If your investment wins, you stand to make only 50 percent. A backer is very vulnerable unless he backs a pool player who's not only honest but who seldom loses. Not too many hustlers meet both criteria.

CHOKER CHARLEY

Though everybody "chokes" to a degree at one time or another, there are certain players who invariably seem to be unable to come through in the clutch. At a critical point in a match, when they know that if they pocket the next ball they'll probably run out, but if they miss it their opponent will probably go all the way, there are some players who always miss. Consequently, they lose the big games, and, in some cases, this is the only thing that keeps them from being top-notch players.

You can't *wish* choking out of your system. But you can take steps to combat it. When you're faced with a critical shot, survey the situation as well as you can and then make the decision and get the shot over with as soon as possible. This doesn't mean you should rush the shot, just that you shouldn't agonize over it. The more you procrastinate, the more pain you put yourself through and the more likely you are to blow the shot.

Some players are terrific when they're in the lead and they face an important shot. But the same competitors just melt if the game is close or they're trailing in the same situation. Others (myself included) are lucky enough to like to play under pressure. The tighter the situation and the more important the shot, the better we do.

If you tend to choke up when the going gets tough, just try to get yourself going faster, without dwelling on how tight a spot you're in.

NERVOUS NORM

You'll find players who show nervousness through herky-jerky body motions and even facial tics, but sometimes what appears to be a sign of nervousness isn't. A player by the name of Edgar White was nicknamed "Shake 'n Bake" for the way he constantly jumped around and shook when he played pool. But that was just his style. He was constantly in motion, pacing, talking to other players and spectators, not because he was worried but because of nervous energy he had in abundance. That was his way of trying to relax. Players who always stay in motion usually don't do so to upset their opponents; it's just their natural style.

BODY-ENGLISH BOB

A cousin to Nervous Norm is Body-English Bob, who uses body motion to try to direct balls where he wants them to go, after he's made the shot.

Arthur Cranfield really qualified as both types. He'd shoot and do pirouettes and other kinds of movements, as if they had any control over what was already in motion on the pool table. One time he spun around to help the ball, and the butt of his cue stick caught the referee, Al Gassner, on the side of the head and knocked him cold. And nervous? In one match that we played to 75 points I think he went through five packs of cigarettes. At one point he had four cigarettes lit at one time. That's nervous.

Dave The Face was a famous twister and spinner, and a current player, called Leapin' Lillis, runs from one end of the table to the other, jumping as he goes, to make the balls go in a particular direction. These guys are real crowd pleasers.

If you're a Body-English Bob, that's fine. But don't think your bodily gyrations have any effect on the shot you've just taken. It doesn't mean a thing once you've taken your swing.

COOL-HAND LUKE

While some players are constantly in motion, seemingly a bundle of nerve endings, others are closer to the icewater-in-the-veins species. With some, this exterior calm is deliberate—Ray Martin, for one, who's called "Cool Cat."

No doubt, some of these icewater players feel it gives them an advantage over an opponent who may be thinking, "I'm nervous as anything, and this guy is cool as ice." But the only thing that really intimidates an opponent is your ability to put ball after ball into the pocket.

So it's fine if you're naturally cool, but don't fake it, hoping to fool.

FLAMBOYANT FREDDIE

A few of the top players like to dress out of the ordinary. For example, even when they're playing in a tournament that doesn't require tuxedos, Pat Fleming will wear a brown one and Lou Butera, who's called the "White Knight" by some of his opponents, will wear a white one. Dapper dressing may be good for the player's and fans' morale, but it has no bearing on the game, unless it's too tight to permit fluid stroking.

RAUNCHY RODNEY

At the other end of poolroom dress are the Raunchy Rodneys, the filthy-looking guys who wear torn T-shirts and jeans and have holes in their shoes.

Worse than their dress, though, are their playing habits. They'll do anything to win, such as spit in your chalk or *shark* you by deliberately waving a white handkerchief in your line of vision when you're about to make a shot. They'll also call undeserved fouls when there is no official presiding at your match.

OVERCONFIDENT OTTO

Overconfident Otto thinks he's so much better than his opponent that he gives him too much of a handicap; or, when he gets a big lead, he slacks off and ends up either losing or barely eking out a win when he should have run away with the game. Guys of this type may also take less of a handicap than they should because of their overconfident feelings.

Overconfidence has cost many a player a game or a bet. Self-confidence is vital; overconfidence can get you in the vitals.

BET-A-BUNDLE BEN

There's a hard-luck story for every cue on the pool hall wall, and some of the saddest involve the guys who have $530 to their name, with the room rent due the next day, and no idea of where their next buck is coming from. These are the fellows who then bet $500 on a pocket billiards game.

By overbetting their bankroll, they put extra pressure on

themselves. Losing now means not only kissing the $500 goodbye but maybe facing eviction as well.

Some players who bet too much think it's a way of intimidating their opponent. But often, the situation turns out to resemble a poker game with a lot of bluffing by one player. He finds out, to his chagrin, that the guy he's trying to bluff has not only the dollars to call the bet but the cards to win it.

Work hard to control that impulse to bet more than you can afford to lose.

WILD WALLY/SPACEMAN SPENCER

Sometimes a player who can't attract attention through good pool playing does it with some wild antics. This unpredictable type will shoot at anything on the table and bet any amount, whether he can afford it or not. He's liable to come into the pool hall loaded, a girl on either arm, and then leave them and jump over the table for no good reason. He plays terribly, but he gets the attention he wants, even though it's negative.

Rather than be counted as a "nut case," concentrate your energies on improving your game.

SLOWPOKE SAMMY

One of the most irritating types of players you're likely to encounter in a billiard parlor is the one who takes forever to select his shot, aim, and finally shoot. It's seldom a deliberate tactic to drive you crazy, but it does have that effect.

In tournaments there are time limits for each shot, and if you take too long, the referee can call a foul. But the time limit is something like three minutes a shot, which is an awfully long time when you're the player sitting down.

If you're in that unfortunate situation, all you can do is meditate or tell yourself jokes. And if you're the slowpoke, you want to make sure that taking so much time for each shot isn't building up anxiety within you and hurting your chances of making your shot.

HOTDOG HERBIE

Like a certain player who shows off in a certain well-known beer commercial on television, some players are always hotdogging. They strut around, bow to the crowd, giggle—the whole bit. I laugh and joke with the crowd, but, unlike the Hotdog Herbies, I'm not sarcastic or phony in my carrying on. Those who are too cocky lose track of what they're really there to do—they're there to play pool, not to tell the crowd how good they are.

JOVIAL JACK

Joviality is a nice trait in anyone, even a pool player; but if it's carried to an extreme, it can hurt your play. If you're too jovial, you might not be sufficiently serious or concentrate as you should to play winning pool. I know a lot of players, who, if they calmed down a little and were a little less jovial or flamboyant, would be much better players than they are.

7

TOURNAMENTS I'VE PLAYED AND LESSONS I'VE LEARNED

There are few things a veteran pool player likes more than to recall games or matches that meant a lot to his career. Count me among that group.

But because this is an instruction book, I'm going to tell you about competitions of mine that not only were thrills (or chills) for me but have some instructional value for you—examples of what you should or should not do.

My first major tournament, which I mentioned earlier, was the "TV Tournament of Champions," held at the Elgin (Illinois) Country Club. That program was part of a successful 13-week series that ran for five years.

As a 17-year-old, I was flattered to have been asked to the invitational tournament along with 15 other players, including such seasoned veterans as Joey Canton, Arthur Cranfield, and Irving Crane. It was through Willie Mosconi (who, with Chris Schenkel, was the TV commentator) that I was invited.

I was scheduled to play my first match at night and spent the afternoon watching some of the others. The level of play that afternoon was poor, and I remember asking Irving Crane, "How come nobody's playing well?"

"After you get out there and play your first match," he said, "come back and tell me how well *you* played."

As you can imagine, I kept quiet after that, but—as luck would have it—I played very well and won my first match, against either Jimmy Caras or Joey Canton. The pockets had been tightened up to 4½ inches, and the TV people offered an extra bonus prize to anyone who ran 75-and-out. With the pockets that tight, they weren't in much danger of having to award bonuses. In my first game I managed a run of 55, which I think was high for the whole tournament.

The match I remember most in that tournament was against Frank McGown in a three-way playoff to determine who would be in the finals. After Crane clinched a spot it came down to a point at which I had to hold McGown to 31 points or less while I scored 75. If he ended with better than 31, he'd get into the finals, even if I beat him.

Playing extremely well, I had him buried and was one point from winning the match. The 75th ball was a hanger, an easy straight-in shot, but I hurried—and missed! To say I was hysterical would be an understatement. I was frantic. The veteran players at the tournament couldn't believe I had blown such an easy shot, and neither could I. Now it was only a matter of time, I feared, before McGown would run out or reach the total he needed. For though he had only about 15 points, a player of his caliber would have little trouble making a run of 18 or better. I blacked out.

Somehow, luck was still with me. On my missed shot, the cue ball came over to the side rail, caromed off another rail, and left Frank snookered.

He had a couple of choices, both bad. For one ball he would have had to shoot the length of the table, over a ball that was almost frozen to the rail. Or he could try to pocket the ball I had jawed in the hole, but he couldn't see it.

Although I had fainted from the shock of muffing the hanger, I was able to see the situation that confronted my opponent because, just as I drew a blank, the TV people called a time-out to reload their film cameras. By the time they were ready to go again, I had revived.

McGown surveyed the table carefully and then decided to gamble. He took a carom off the short rail but missed the object ball by a foot. My heartbeat accelerated, and it raced even more when the cue ball stopped only 12 inches away from the object ball I had goofed up on. It was still hanging right in front of the pocket.

I swore I wasn't going to mess up this opportunity. I approached the table quickly. Then, remembering what rushing had done to me the last time up, I deliberately went back to the chair, filed the tip of my cue stick a little bit, chalked up, and went back to the table. I looked at the shot that even a 2-year-old could have made, but which a 17-year-old had missed, and went back to the chair another time. I powdered my hands to make sure the cue would move smoothly through them, then drank some 7-Up and went over and made the shot.

The moral of the story is obvious: Take your time. Don't act too hastily. Be sure of every shot, no matter how easy it may seem to be. My problem was that it was so easy, I took everything for granted, except missing it. On my second chance, I may have taken a lot more time than necessary, but I think that's understandable in view of what had happened with it the first time.

After my victory in that semifinal match I was so shaken from the missed shot that I was a nervous wreck. I had an hour and a half in which to get over it before the final match against Irving Crane. But I didn't get over it. He played well and easily defeated me, 75 to about 32.

As runner-up in the tournament, I won $3,500, which was a tremendous amount of money to a 17-year-old in his first major competition. Had I come in first, I would have won $5,000, and had I failed to keep McGown under 31 points in the semifinal, I would have won about $2,500—so that missed shot could have cost me about a thousand dollars.

It's worth repeating: take your time *on every shot.*

My overall performance in the "TV Tournament of Champions" spurred me on to play well, and I was invited to the World Championship (sponsored by the Billiard Room Proprietors) the next year.

Probably the youngest player in that competition, I was undefeated after the third day, along with two other players, and was the hit, the hot player, of the tournament.

Then I came up against Cowboy Jimmy Moore, a husky, white-haired man in his 40s, from Albuquerque, New Mexico. The 5-foot 10-inch competitor, who wore cowboy hat, boots, and tie, was quite a sight—and quite a player.

That day, though, I ran off to a big lead, 132–21, in a 150-point game and had the attitude that the game was over. Well, as you might have guessed, I missed a shot, and he started pocketing balls with the sure-handedness of a cowpoke lassoing cattle. Sweating, swearing, almost wetting my pants, I squirmed in my chair, hoping that he would trip or that lightning would strike the table, but Cowboy kept running balls for an hour. He made 121 in a row! Then *he* missed, and it was my turn. Now trailing Jimmy 143–132, I was in shooting distance of victory, but his rally had crushed my spirit and left me so nervous, shaken, and disgusted that I missed my first shot. He went on to win the game.

Walking out of the tournament building, the old Commodore Hotel in New York City, I began crying. As an 18-year-old, I was behaving like a kid who had just had his toy abruptly taken away from him. I asked my father to get Cowboy Jimmy and bring him over to me, and while he did, I sat in a corner of the hotel, bawling my eyes out.

"What's the matter, Mizzy?" Cowboy asked me.

"I don't mind you beating me," I answered, tears still rolling down my cheek, "but did you have to beat me that way?" Remember, I was a teenager, with an awesome lead in the game and a solid chance to win the tournament. And then he came back so strong that he shook me up and left me nervous as hell, so nervous I couldn't score again. I was upset with him and, mostly, with myself.

Jimmy leaned over me and said, softly but firmly, "Son, it's not the first game you ever lost, and it's not the last game you'll ever lose. That was a tough one to lose, but you're going to lose games worse than that. And another thing: Remember that for every game you lose like that you're going to beat somebody the same way. So it all comes out in the wash."

The message? Take your losses—and your victories—philosophically. And, when an opponent makes a tremendous comeback in a match, the way Cowboy Jimmy did, don't let it shake you so much that your own play is ruined. Maybe it's just homely philosophy, but it makes sense, in life as well as at the pool table: you're going to win some and lose some, and either way, the sun's going to rise tomorrow.

Incidentally, that was the first time I had played Jimmy Moore, and, for a while, it seemed to set a pattern. The next year we met in the World Championship in California, and he ran 65 from the break to lead me 65-0. The next shot, I got off to a run of 132 before missing. Then he ran 85-and-out.

For about four consecutive tournaments I considered him my jinx. Although he played well consistently, part of my losing was psychological. "Why does this son-of-a-gun have to play well whenever he plays me?" I'd ask myself, and the feeling that he had my number probably affected my own playing. But as I became more seasoned I learned how to cope with that seeming psychological edge he had on me, and I started to beat him.

Possibly my greatest thrill was winning my first U.S. Open title. The tournament took place in the grand ballroom of the Sheraton-Chicago Hotel. When I met Luther Lassiter, then a pocket billiards legend, in the final match, the ballroom was packed with about 2,000 spectators.

I broke—and did it perfectly. Luther took a scratch, and so did I. We played safe back and forth, taking about three back-scratches each. Then I caught a shot and began running balls—80, 90, 100. I thought I was running out. But at

105 I broke the balls and was left with a very tough shot. The cue ball made its way up the table, through seven balls, down the table through the others, and the object ball went in. But the cue ball scratched in the corner.

So now the score was 101 to his *minus* 3, and it was his turn again. Luther began running balls and got to 85 before calling a time-out to go to the bathroom. When he came back he had a perfect break shot, but he missed, hitting the cue ball right into the rail. I got up and began picking off balls and ran 49-and-out. The championship was mine.

I sat there and cried, but this time my tears were tears of happiness. "What are you crying about?" people yelled. It was just that I was happy, and in those days crying was one way I showed my emotions. That victory was especially memorable and meaningful, because it came at a time when I was very young and my career was just starting to grow.

The 1971 U.S. Open came down to Joe Balsis, the most feared pocket billiards player of that time, and me. I won the winner's side—no losses in a tournament where you had to be defeated twice to be eliminated. This meant Joe would have to beat me twice to win, but that wasn't a particularly consoling thought because, most of the time, when someone is able to beat you once he can beat you twice.

Joe got off to a big lead, 98–2, in a match being played to 150. Then I got hot and brought my score to 103. I think I would have been able to go all the way, but at 103 I had to shoot over a ball, and I fouled. In championship play, if you hit another ball with anything other than your cue tip, you lose your turn, and that's what happened. This was the match in which the only person to see me foul was the referee, but he was the guy who counted. The TV camera didn't pick it up, but no matter; I had lost my turn.

Balsis got up and started running balls, and I thought, "This could be it," but at 17 he missed, and I was able to run 47-and-out. It was a real upset, which naturally made me feel awfully good. And it drove home a lesson that would keep coming up again and again: the game is never over until the last ball is made. When I was down 98-2 it would have been easy to throw in the towel. But, luckily, I didn't— and I managed to win.

I won the next two Open championships, but they were both lackluster or worse. After defeating Danny DiLiberto in 1972 I played Luther Lassiter in 1973 in a pair of matches that were so terrible that I think they drove Straight Pool off television. Luther beat me in the first game; then I came back and beat him. We both played so badly that each game took about four hours. Fortunately, in the second game he played a little worse than I did. I can't tell you what made those matches so poor; chalk it up to circumstances beyond our control.

In the course of the next five years or so there were other times when circumstances seemed to be out of control, but never so weirdly as in the first Professional Pool Players Association (PPPA) World Open that I won, in 1979.

From about 1975 to 1978 I'd been having trouble winning tournaments, partly because of a lot of personal problems. For some reason, too, I did not play well in televised matches, not that TV scared me. It just happened.

In 1978 I began playing well again, and when the PPPA finals came around in 1979 I was matched against Danny DiLiberto. Thinking about the match, I felt that, if I could get off to a lead, I'd be able to hold it.

The match was moving along fine, as far as I was concerned, until suddenly strange things began to happen on the table. I played position for one ball, planning to go two rails, but the ball just flew off and ended up going seven rails! Here it was a match of supposed championship caliber, and we weren't able to control the cue ball. We'd put draw on it, and it would follow. The object balls were acting funny, jumping instead of rolling. Everything was freakish—the speed, the rails, position, everything. It was an oddity that I had never seen before and haven't seen since. If you ran 14, you were doing a lot.

Anyway, I didn't let the mysterious change in the equipment—which may have been due to a combination of people, the TV lights, and the weather outside—affect me, and I won the match and the championship. What made the victory so satisfying for me was that people had begun to think I couldn't play anymore. Many of them were thinking of me as a has-been, and a lot of them were envious of me because of my affiliation with Miller Lite and the TV commercials, so they'd been sort of pleased that I'd been having trouble winning matches. Sometimes some of the players and fans were downright rude and discourteous, whispering or even yelling insults.

So this victory was psychologically very important to me. It's customary for the victor to throw a little celebration, and when one of the players who'd been putting me down asked, "Where's the party?" I said, "The party's only for my friends."

There were a couple of lessons to be learned from this tournament. The big one, I suppose, was that you should never give up on yourself. After the long famine I'd experienced in tournament victories, it was tempting to say goodbye to my career. But I didn't, and I started winning again.

The other moral was that you can't let quirks of equipment or circumstances, no matter how weird, throw you. The strange way the table and balls were reacting did scramble our brains a little, but neither Danny DiLiberto nor I let it hopelessly screw up our game. This was a little different from the year before, when I did let an equipment problem affect me.

It happened in the PPPA World Open, when I was playing Nick Varner. Just as I was getting ready to play, the tip fell off my cue stick because of the type of glue that was on it. I had another shaft, which didn't have a tip I liked, but I had to use it, until Allen Hopkins went upstairs and used superglue to paste the tip back on the shaft I'd planned to use. He got the shaft back to me about halfway through the game. The contest was a close one that I lost, even with the shaft I preferred. I think the effect of the tip falling off was enough to upset me to the point that it made a difference in the outcome of the game. Nick beat me twice, and I finished third in the tournament.

This is not to take anything away from Nick, who is a great player and one of the few really good guys competing. The point I want to make, though, is that when something goes wrong with your equipment you have to make the best of it; you can't let it upset you. And, of course, you should do your best to keep your equipment in tip-top shape.

The victory over Danny DiLiberto marked a return to winning ways for me. The next year I won the PPPA World Open from Jimmy Fusco, who had never played in a televised match before. As an up-and-coming player, he was the focus of attention, and I think that being in the limelight, coupled with awareness of the TV cameras, cost him, as did the pressure of being in the finals of a Straight Pool tournament. Straight Pool is not his game. It was really no surprise that I was able to blast him out.

I'm proud to say that since the PPPA tournament started, through 1983, at least, I'm the only player who has ever shot a so-called "perfect game"—150-and-out. I've done it twice.

The first time I accomplished the feat was against Rusty Miller in Asbury Park, the New Jersey Atlantic Coast resort. My performance really defied some adverse circumstances, beginning with a sleepless night before the match. The tournament took place in the summer, but the air conditioning in the motel I stayed in wasn't functioning right, so I tossed and turned most of the night. Toward morning I finally fell asleep, only to be awakened by an early call to come over to the Convention Center for an interview a half-hour later. So I was bone tired when the match began.

Then partway through the match, a hurricane blew with such force that it knocked over a score screen and sent the balls on the table all over the place. The referee replaced the balls as close to their original positions as he could. Somehow, neither my sleepless night nor the howling hurricane bothered me one bit. I just kept running balls until I hit 150-and-out.

That I was able to perform as well as I did under such bizarre circumstances is due, I think, to the fact that when I come to a pool tournament I come to play pool. I don't go there to do anything else—no drinking, smoking, looking for women, or anything else. I'm there solely to win a pool tournament. That's one of the main reasons I've been able to play pool well for a longer time than most players. And I recommend you do the same. When you go to a pocket billiards room or tournament, concentrate only on the game played on the table, nothing else. Don't let yourself be distracted. And, even though I was able to shoot such a great game on next to no sleep, that's an exception. Get all the rest you need before you play.

Incidentally, players have no say in whether their matches are scheduled for afternoon or evening. For some, the time of day when their contests are scheduled does have an effect on how well they play; some are very definitely "night players." I'm lucky in that, having been a full-time teacher for almost 15 years, I'm used to being bright-eyed and bushy-tailed early in the day. I like nighttime, too, so I can play at any time of day.

Whenever you have a match you intend to play seriously, you have to get yourself in top shape, mentally and physically. I want to do well in every tournament I enter, but certain ones have special meaning for me, so I'm careful to prepare for them by losing some weight and sharpening my eye by practicing four or five hours every day for about a week before the event. The better you prepare for the competition, the less likely you are to have headaches or other symptoms of pressure or tension when you're in the competition.

When the 1983 PPPA World Championship opened in New York City I was really ready. As in any topflight competition in any major sport, say golf or tennis, you figure if you can get through your first couple of matches and get used to the equipment and surroundings, you probably can go all the way.

I started out by beating Rusty Miller, 150–75. Then I played Roy Ruffen, a cop out of Rochester, and beat him, 150 to about 60. Gaining confidence, I played Mike Sigel, with whom I've had a close rivalry over the last few years. I beat him with a tight game and then went against the hottest stick in the tournament, Bob Vanover, from Texas. Even though he ran 121, I defeated him.

My next opponent was Grady Matthews, a good, solid player, but that night everything was going my way. I ran 129 to take over the high-run position in the tournament and won, 150–1. I won another match, which put me into the semifinals. My opponent again was Grady, who, except for our first match, had been playing very strong pool.

The semifinals took place on Friday night in front of a packed house. Ray Martin and Jimmy Fusco were playing on the other table. The winner of that match would play the winner of the contest between Grady Matthews and me the following afternoon.

I broke, and Grady made the first shot; I was convinced I was in for a tough evening. But suddenly Grady got himself hooked without a clear shot. He tried something and missed, and it was my turn. I kept running balls without a hitch. No tough shots, not even a thought of missing. And, as it turned out, I wasn't being overconfident—because, in what has been described as a "picture-perfect" run, I pocketed 150 balls in a row, running out and into the finals. People told me afterward that it was the best pool they had ever seen in their lives; they had never seen balls run so perfectly. Why it happened, I can't really explain, except that I'd been playing well throughout the tournament, and in that game everything came together just right.

The final match against Jimmy Fusco was really no contest. I was still riding high from my semifinals "perfect" game, but the game got off to a slow start, with the two of us exchanging safeties for the first four or five shots. Then Jimmy missed, and I built up a 124 to *minus* 2 lead. I really felt I had him, and the temptation was to let down. But, as an old veteran who has experienced victories and losses in games that shaped up as "sure things" the other way, I knew it was dangerous to let a player like Jimmy off the hook. I kept concentrating until I had my 150 and the championship.

In each of the contests I've described there are lessons to be learned. They taught me things about the game, including psychological aspects of it, and I hope they've done the same for you. Some of the morals are principles I stressed earlier in the book, but they bear repeating—and absorbing—especially if you're going to improve from beginner to advanced level.

ABOUT
STEVE MIZERAK

1970 ⎤
1971 ⎥ United States Open Champion
1972 ⎥
1973 ⎦

1970 ⎤
1971 ⎥
1972 ⎥ Billiard News Open Champion
1973 ⎥
1974 ⎦

1967 ⎤
1968 ⎥
1969 ⎥
1970 ⎥
1972 ⎥ New Jersey State Champion
1973 ⎥
1974 ⎥
1977 ⎦

1966 Indiana State Champion

1968 Empire Billiards Association Cavalcade of Stars

1969 Salt City Open—Syracuse, New York

1969
1970 } Norfolk Invitational

1970
1973 } United States Masters—Arlington, Virginia
1976

1970
1977 } Pool Consultant for the Brunswick Corporation

1970 Stardust Open—Las Vegas

1971 Michigan Open
United States Masters 9 Ball
New York City Metropolitan

1972 Michigan Open
Norwick Union Challenge Cup—London, England

1973 Michigan Open
Kentucky Classic
Norfolk Invitational
Kingston Invitational
Eastern States Classic—New York

1974 United States Masters
Pabst Brunswick Pro Tour—Ohio State University
Pabst Brunswick Pro Tour—Penn State University

Pabst Brunswick Pro Tour—University of
Tennessee

Pabst Brunswick Pro Tour—Florida State
University

1975 United States Masters

Empire State Open

High Q Masters

1977 New York State 14.1 Champion

World Series of Pool

New Jersey State Champion, 9 Ball

St. Louis Open

1978 Pool Consultant for Phoenix Theater's off-Broadway
play, "One Crack Out"

Norfolk Invitational

Trick & Tough Shot Champion—the Waldorf Astoria

Trick & Tough Shot Champion—Las Vegas

1979 Miller Lite commercial, "Just Showing Off"

Legendary Pool Players' Showdown, "ABC Wide
World of Sports"

United States Open, 9 Ball

1980 Breaker Pool 14.1 Challenge Cup—Manchester,
England

Eastern States, 9 Ball

Miller Lite commercial, "Practice, Practice,
Practice"

Advisory Director, Adam Custom Cues (*through
1982*)

8-Ball World Invitational, "CBS Sports Spectacular"—Lake Tahoe

Team Championship, "CBS Sports Spectacular"—Lake Tahoe

9-Ball Championship held prior to appearance in movie with James Coburn and Omar Sharif, *The Baltimore Bullet*

Youngest pool player ever inducted into the Billiards Congress of America Hall of Fame

1981   Team Championship, "CBS Sports Spectacular"—Las Vegas

Miller Lite Christmas commercial

1982   MC for Miller Lite $200,000 World Series of Tavern Pool Tour

Florida Open, 9-Ball Tournament Champion—Melbourne, Florida

Team Championship, "CBS Sports Spectacular"—Atlantic City

Legends vs. New Legends, "CBS Sports Spectacular"—Atlantic City

Eastern States Straight Pool Tournament—New London, Connecticut

World Pocket Billiards Champion—Roosevelt Hotel, New York

1983   9-Ball Open Champion—Houston, Texas

BBIA Man of the Year Award—St. Petersburg, Florida

Q-Masters Billiards 9-Ball Champion—Norfolk, Virginia

Legends-to-Be (Mizerak and Hopkins) beat Legends
(Mosconi and Fats) at 7 Ball and 9 Ball—
Caesars, Atlantic City

Beat World 9-Ball Champion Allen Hopkins at 7 ball
and 9 ball to become the Undisputed Pocket
Billiards World Champion—Caesars, Atlantic
City

Billiard Shootout Champion on television's "That's
Incredible"

World Pocket Billiards Champion for second
consecutive year—Roosevelt Hotel, New York

INDEX

Albany Billiard Company, 16

Balabushka, George, 3
Balkline Carom Championship, 42
Balls, 16–17; care of, 17; trouble, 83, 92, 106, *illus.* 84, 107–112
Balsis, Joe, 164–65
Bank shot, 35, 53, 89, 125, 127–28, *illus.* 90
Betting, 117–18, 120–21, 142, 153–54
Billiard games. *See* Five-Ahead, 14.1 Continuous Billiards, Hit-the-Ball, Nine-Ball, One-Pocket, One-Shootout, Race to 10, Ring Nine-Ball, Straight Pool, Three-Cushion Billiards
Billiard room proprietors, 161
Break ball, 48–49, 92–94, 95

Breaks: in Eight-Ball, 54; in Nine-Ball, 50–52, *illus.* 50; in Straight Pool, 75–78, opening, 42–46; safe, 53
Bridges, *illus.* 18–19; artificial, 2; mechanical, 17–20, 33; open, *illus.* 29–31; open vs. closed, 28–32
Brunswick Centennials, 16
Brunswick of Chicago, 12
Brunswick's Gold Crown, 12
Butera, Lou, 60, 150

Call Shot. *See* Straight Pool
Canfield, Arthur, 159
Canton, Joey, 159, 160
Caras, Jimmy, 160
Caroms, 34–35, 53, 89, *illus.* 34, 91; one-cushion, 28
Chalk: brands, 8; usage, 8–10, *illus.* 9

Chenier, George, 28
Choking, 145
Combination shot, 33, 35-36, 56, *illus.* 35-36
Crane, Irving, 60, 62, 63, 117, 159, 161
Cranfield, Arthur, 64, 147-48
Crutch, 17
Cue ball: floating, 100; placement of, 132; run wild, 83-87, 100, *illus.* 86
Cue stick, 1-5; case, 5-6; furl, 10; grip, 23; one-piece vs. two-piece, 1-2, 1-2; practice strokes, 26; stroking, 23-28, *illus.* 25; tip, 6-7; wrap, 11

Dave the Face, 148
DiLiberto, Danny, 165-66
Draw, 33, 46-47, 95

Eight-Ball, 54-56, 62, 129-35, *illus.* 130-31; opening break, 129-32
English, 87, 95, 132, *illus.* 133; left-hand, 33, 124; right-hand, 33-34, 43; used in opening break, 74-78, *illus.* 75

Five-Ahead, 49-50
Fleming, Pat, 150
Floating cue ball, 100
14.1 Continuous Pocket Billiards, 41-49. *See also* Straight Pool
Follow, 33
Follow shot, 28, *illus.* 28-31
Foot spot, 43
Foul, 139, 156

Frozen, 34, 47-48, 78, 83, 95, 98-100, 121-24, *illus.* 79, 99
Fusco, Jimmy, 61, 167, 169-70

Gandy's Big G, 12
Gandy's National Brand, 8
Gassner, Al, 147-48
Grip, 23, *illus.* 24

Handicaps, 139, 143
Head rail, 104
Head spot, 49, 78
Helmsteader, Dick, 3
Hemple, Bob, 6
Hit-the-Ball, 52. *See also* Nine-Ball
Hitting, 59, 95-97, *illus.* 96-97
Hitting cue ball: draw, 33; follow, 33. *See also* English
Hopkins, Allen, 57-58, 59-60, 61, 64, 100-4, 117, 118, 166
Hustlers, 120-21

James, Danny, 3

Key ball, 48, 92
Kicks, 113
Kisses. *See* Caroms

La Professional, 7
Lag, 42
Lagenlacher, Erich, 42-43
Lane, Dick, 68-69
Laurie, Onofrio, 58-64
Leaning, 14
Lassiter, Luther, 163-64, 165
Leisure World's Trafalgar, 12
Lillis, Leapin', 148

Martin, Ray, 148, 169
Masters chalk, 8
Matthews, Grady, 61, 169
McGown, Frank, 160
Michigan Open, 68
Miller, Rusty, 167, 169
Moore, Cowboy Jimmy, 162
Mosconi, Willie, 159

Nine-Ball, 49–53, 61, 62, *illus.*
    115–16; opening break,
    98–104, *illus.* 99, 101–3;
    playing safe, 117; scratching,
    120, *illus.* 120; strategy,
    104–6

One-Pocket, 52, 54, 61, 121–28,
    illus. 122–23; opening break
    in, 121–24
One-Shot Shootout, 52, 120. *See
    also* Nine-Ball
Opening break. *See* Call Shot,
    Nine-Ball, One-Pocket, One-
    Shot Shootout, Straight Pool
Overpracticing, 58

Playing safe, 47–48, 51, 83, 106,
    117, *illus.* 85
Pockets, 89
Position, 37–39, *illus.* 37–38
Position play, 78–82, *illus.* 79–82
Powder, 10, 65
Practice, 58, 72, 113
Professional Pool Players
    Association (PPPA) World
    Open, 16, 165–70

Race to 10, 119
Riggie, Richard, 64
Ring Nine-Ball, 52

Ruffen, Roy, 169
Running out, 48
Russo Interlocking Bridge, 17
Russo, Joe, 17

Safeties. *See* Playing safe
Schaefer, Jake, Jr., 42–43
Schriver, Earl, 142–43
Scoring, 59–60
Scratching, 46–48, 51, 56, 113,
    132; on opening break,
    43–46, 120; on purpose,
    47–48
Shaft, weight, 3
Shooting: over a ball, 32; with
    mechanical bridge 17–20.
    See also Stroking
Sharking, 151
Sigel, Mike, 62, 117, 169
Slip stroke, 23
Snookering, 39, 113, 118, 160
Spotting, 43–46
Stance, 21–23, *illus.* 22
Straight Pool, 61, 70–71; opening
    break in, 43–46, *illus.* 44–45,
    75–78; position in, 37
Strategy, 79–82; in Eight-Ball,
    133–35, *illus.* 134; in One-
    Pocket, 124–28; on the
    break, 51–52
Stroking: follow-through, 28;
    intensity, 28, *illus.* 26, 27;
    practice strokes, 26. *See
    also* Shooting
Stroud, Bill, 3
Szamboti, Gus, 3

Tables, 12–16, *illus.* 40
Three-Cushion Billiards, 113
Time limits, 156
Trouble spots, 83
True Speed Rubber, 15

TV Tournament of Champions,
   159-62

U.S. Open, 163-65

Vanover, Bob, 169
Varner, Nick, 166-67

White, Edgar, 146